KU-560-483

How To Read
Scottish Buildings

Daniel MacCannell is married with one daughter and lives in Levenhall, East Lothian, where he runs The Historical Detective Agency Ltd. He has studied Scottish, English, Dutch and French buildings, landscapes and townscapes for more than twenty years, and was awarded a PhD in History and Art History by the University of Aberdeen in 2010. He is the great-grandson of Canadian-American landscape architect Earle Edgerly MacCannell.

2

How to Read Scottish Buildings

Daniel MacCannell

First published in
Great Britain in 2015 by
Birlinn Ltd
West Newington House
10 Newington Road
Edinburgh
EH9 1QS

www.birlinn.co.uk

ISBN: 978 1 78027 118 7

Copyright © Daniel MacCannell 2015

The right of Daniel MacCannell to
be identified as the author of this work
has been asserted by him in accordance
with the Copyright, Designs and
Patents Act, 1988

All rights reserved. No part of this
publication may be reproduced, stored,
or transmitted in any form, or by any
means, electronic, mechanical or
photocopying, recording or otherwise,
without the express written
permission of the publisher.

British Library Cataloguing-in-Publication Data
A catalogue record for this book is available
from the British Library

Designed and typeset by Mark Blackadder

Printed and bound by Gutenberg Press Ltd, Malta

Dedicated by permission to

Sir Moir Lockhead of Glassel and Lady Lockhead,
whose early and continuing encouragement of
my interest in Scotland's remarkable architectural
heritage made this book possible

and to

Anna Brown,
its ideal reader

Contents

I
Introduction

This is not a book about buildings that are famous. Cathedrals, palaces and royal castles will be mentioned only in passing. I do not need to explain how to tell the difference between Hopetoun House and the Waverley Gate office building (both illus. p. 130), because if you are reading this book, you can certainly read road signs. Rather, this is a book for and about the many thousands of curious, attractive, sometimes even beautiful old Scottish buildings for which there are no plaques, no websites, no costumed guides or colourful pamphlets or 'ancient monument' categorisations. For the most part, the names of the people who designed and built them are forgotten. Their styles may be unnamed or disputed, their exact ages unrecorded, their initial purposes fading from memory. And yet they enfold us, complementing and perhaps equalling the beauty and intrigue of our mountains, lakes, rivers and forests.

Most writing about this compelling subject is overly technical – an alphabet soup of L-plans, Z-plans and bartizans – or pushes some tendentious political, architectural or historical agenda: such-and-such an era was not violent, such-and-such a family was not Francophile and so forth. Instead, this book is intended to provide travellers and residents with an impartial, brief, clearly illustrated guide that allows them to place Scottish buildings and groups of buildings with regard to their ages, styles, influences and functions, as well as the messages that their builders, owners and occupants intended them to convey. I hope it will enable you to deduce for yourself – unassisted by massive foliosized volumes, personal tour guides or an expensive degree course – what you are looking at. How old is this? What sort of people probably built it, and for what purpose? Does its style have a name? Is it an outstanding, typical, or inferior example? Might it have been designed by, or in imitation of, a famous architect? Is it a 'marriage' of older and newer elements – or purely a revival of an older style? Why might it have been built in this position, and not somewhere else? How much, if anything, does this structure owe to the influence of French, English, Italian, Spanish, Flemish, Dutch, Nordic and other Scottish buildings (and pictures of buildings)?

Unlike other books on Scottish architecture, this one is not divided by region; and rather than shoehorning building styles into reigns or dynasties, it divides Scottish architecture into six stylistic eras that arise naturally from the appearance of the buildings themselves. Fundamentally, it is a book to be used whilst walking around; and buildings of every conceivable age, style and purpose occur cheek-by-jowl in every part of the country. As with the example of Hopetoun and Waverley Gate, you will *already know* whether you have stopped your car in the Highlands or Fife, or Jedburgh or Peterhead. Accordingly, *Understanding Scottish Buildings* teaches a deductive approach that can be applied equally well to Scottish buildings in any setting. Eventually, as you travel about the country making your own observations, you will see considerable regional variation, some of which is touched on in these pages and some of which is not. The important thing is to keep looking; for as Paul Cézanne reminded us, specifically with regard to the buildings of his native Aix-en-Provence: 'You will have to hurry if you want to see anything. Everything is disappearing.'[1]

There are two key skills that any analyst of Scottish buildings must master, and which this book endeavours to teach you. The first is the quick mental partitioning of a building into its parts, including – if it is a large, complicated building – a willingness to see it as two, or three, or even more different buildings that happen to have been built close together; and then to analyse *those* buildings according to *their* parts. This technique will be explained in greater depth in the pages that follow, via a series of concrete examples. But before the technique can be of much use, it is necessary to get a handle on the six major epochs of Scottish buildings, in terms of style, size and construction techniques. This does *not* proceed according to centuries, monarchical/dynastic reigns, or named styles from other countries, but arises solely from close observation of our own country's buildings, towns and villages themselves.

Since the year 1371 we have had only two dynasties, each of them simply too long to be architecturally significant in itself; and at 116 years, even the Georgian age is too lengthy to be anything other than a grid that we impose artificially over a very diverse set of real buildings in real places. Individual monarchs, meanwhile, often had very short reigns, and only two – James V (*r.* 1513–42) and Charles II (*r.* 1660–85) – had the sort of direct impact on the development of Scottish architecture that one might expect. Named styles like 'Palladianism' are also fairly useless for our purposes, because they filtered out of their countries of origin only very slowly, and in any case were never adopted by the majority of builders in this or any other country. Lastly, categorisation of Scottish building styles by *century* is particularly unhelpful, since in every century from the sixteenth onwards, the great stylistic watershed occurred more or less in the middle of the century, not at the beginning or the end.[2]

Our first and most natural reactions to a building of average size are usually to its colour, texture and condition. To understand it, however, we must teach ourselves to ignore these things initially, since all three can be so readily and rapidly changed. The coatings known as 'harl', 'harling' or 'render' (see section 2–1) were applied to most Scottish stone buildings up to 1750, and many later ones; but these are expensive to maintain and are frequently removed. At the other end of the spectrum, many newly built structures are given such coatings, to blend in with traditional town-scapes – or to fool us into thinking they are old, and/or made of stone, when in fact they may not be. In an ideal world, traditional lime render should be completely replaced every twenty years or so, at which time the pigment (which is mixed directly into it) can be changed completely; there-fore, colour should not generally be used as a clue to a building's age, purpose or influences either. However, if a building has very smooth stone window-surrounds that protrude quite far from a much rougher stone surface, it has almost certainly had its render removed; and as such, it is probably pre-Victorian and possibly pre-Georgian in age. Conversely, a building whose window-surrounds are more or less indistinguishable from the wall-face is likely to date from after rendering ceased to be popular in the late eighteenth century, and before its post-Second World War revival.

Likewise, we should at first ignore signs of decay. Once a building's roof collapses, or is taken off deliberately (as was frequently done for tax purposes in the late 1940s), it deteriorates with alarming rapidity. One can see many Scot-tish country houses built around 1800 and unroofed around 1950 that look in worse shape than certain Ancient Greek remains around the Mediterranean. In other words, smashed windows, boarded-up doorways, partially collapsed walls, trees growing from gutters – sights all too common in our country – are signs of neglect, but not necessarily of anything else. In every case, we must look past the surface to the fundamental design if an accurate reading is to be obtained.

The next chapter provides brief explanations of the

keynotes of architectural style in the six major periods this book will use, as well as *why* these styles changed when they did. From there, we will proceed via some cross-period issues – including styles, and individual buildings, that were built in more than one period – to a more detailed 'top-down' discussion of the most important Scottish building elements, their history and significance, divided into twenty manageable sections. Finally, we provide a set of handy tables that will help you read Scottish buildings on your own, whether in the field, in the library or at home.

2

Getting to Know the
Six Style Periods

2–1
Style before 1540: Middle Ages into Renaissance

Other than castles, palaces, churches and bridges, Scottish buildings from before 1540 are rare as hens' teeth. Authentic contemporary images of them are even rarer. We know that many were built entirely of wood or clay, or a mixture of the two. Those that were built of stone at all often used clay as mortar, or even turf or moss. 'New' Aberdeen has been an inhabited site since the Stone Age, and a chartered town since 1179, but its oldest surviving dwelling is from 1545. This is typical. Even our churches were mostly not built of stone until after the year 1130. Castles, too, were built only of wood and earth up to the thirteenth century (and sometimes into the fourteenth); and these perishable structures survive – if at all – only as earthen mounds known to mapmakers and guidebook-writers as mottes. In this period, only the kings' palaces[3] and the largest churches were built of smooth, carefully worked stone that was intended to be seen;[4] the smaller churches and mere castles were built of rubble and coated with harling (a.k.a. harl or render): a thick, porridge-like weatherproof mixture of lime mortar and pebbles. Harling is naturally off-white, but it can have pigments of almost any colour or shade mixed in.

As roofing materials, straw- and heather thatch were so prevalent that one wealthy landowner of 1520 asked for his castle roof to be 'thatched with lead'. Bridges, too, were mostly of wood and rope before the fifteenth century.

These ephemeral construction techniques, and the reasons they were adopted and abandoned, will be discussed further in the pages that follow. But given the virtual nonexistence of smaller domestic and agricultural structures from before the 1540s, we need not concern ourselves with them just yet.

Noblemen's houses from the end of the earthen-motte period up to 1540 generally took the form of a simple rectangle set on end, made of large stones, with a single door, and few openings that we would recognise as windows. They also tended to lack crenellations, which are described in detail in section 4–3. Though usually upgraded in later centuries, several dozen plain tower-houses of this type survive in relatively unmolested form: for instance, yellow-harled **Liberton Tower** to the south of

Liberton Tower

15

Edinburgh, Lochleven Castle in Kinross and Clackmannan Tower in Clackmannan. 'Curtain' castles of the Anglo-Welsh type made world-famous by David Macaulay's book *Castle* (1977), with multiple gates and round or semi-circular towers connected together in complicated patterns, were rarely built in Scotland. Our best-preserved (albeit still far from habitable) examples, out of just a handful ever built here, are triangular Caerlaverock in Dumfriesshire, circular Rothesay on the Isle of Bute and gigantic Kildrummy in Aberdeenshire, all from the thirteenth century.[5] The Scottish nobility has been, at all periods, poorer than that of England, so building by private individuals on the scale of Warwick Castle has been unusual, to say the least.

The grim, ponderous, almost featureless tower-houses with which the great majority of Scottish noblemen contented themselves became unfashionable in the time of James IV (*r.* 1488–1513) and James V (*r.* 1513–42). This was largely because of these kings' fondness for the style of French chateaux of the Loire and Sarthe regions. As misinterpreted by two generations of Scottish, Italian and Flemish masons working on the royal residences in Holyrood, Falkland, Stirling and elsewhere, French style (including especially crenellations and round towers with 'witch's hat' roofs) and Flemish or Danish touches (e.g. larger windows braced with stone crosses) were subtly transmuted into the style now known as 'Scottish Baronial'. This style, in turn, continued to evolve along its own lines, and came to dominate both our second (1540–1660) and fifth (1840–1920) stylistic epochs.

The realistic approximation of Ancient Roman columns occurred only rarely and sporadically in Scotland up to 1540, with most **medieval columns** being either far fatter relative to their height, or far skinnier relative to their own heads, than their distant Roman ancestors; and where supplied at all, the heads were often carved with a curious

Medieval columns

array of beasts of decidedly un-Roman appearance. The systematic, accurate copying of actual Roman columns first began here *c.* 1540, during the reign and at the behest of King James V, though it was only after 1750 that their use became actually commonplace.

Except for the fact that both have been widened, the Aberdeen Bridge of Dee and the so-called 'Roman' bridge in Musselburgh typify the look of large and small bridges (respectively) of the period 1400–1540. Well into modern times, Scottish bridges of all ages have frequently been destroyed in storms and floods, with the last great weather-related bridge-massacre having occurred in the summer of 1956; so these late-medieval[6] survivors are all the more important. Scottish bridges' key feature, abandoned after the mid seventeenth century, is the use of small triangular or semi-circular projections that allow individuals on foot to stand out of the way of animal-drawn carts. In later eras, bridges were generally wide enough (from new) to allow a man and a cart to pass each other without any such gimmickry.

Here, as in other European countries, the two major styles of churches built before the Protestant Reformation of the mid sixteenth century were Romanesque and Gothic. There are many subtle differences between them, but a church with mostly round-topped windows, doorways and arches is said to be Romanesque and one with mostly pointed windows, doorways and ceiling-vaulting is Gothic. These were not mere preferences, but evolved – Romanesque into Gothic – over the course of the twelfth century. The main influence on original Scottish Romanesque building was Durham Cathedral in the north of England, and this is perhaps most obvious at Dunfermline Abbey in Fife (1130s).

Despite Scotland having been divided into approximately 1,000 parishes from the twelfth century onwards, there is not very much medieval church architecture to be seen. The Gothic movement itself was 'short-lived and weak' in Scotland;[7] churches became military targets from 1378 to 1417 (when the English and Scottish states supported two different rival popes); and a high proportion of Scottish Catholic houses of worship as well as bishops' residences were partially or completely demolished by Protestant mob action in or about 1560. Nevertheless, examples of each type survive. The best include **Dalmeny Church**

Above.
Dalmeny Church

Left.
Glasgow Cathedral

(Romanesque, begun 1130), and **Glasgow Cathedral** (Gothic, begun 1197); with Arbroath Abbey and Coldingham Priory representing a moment of transition between the two styles. Most importantly, for our purposes, these two medieval modes were both revived during our fifth style period – 1840–1920, Scotland's great age of 'retro' architecture – with neo-Gothic being more popular at the beginning of that period, and neo-Romanesque more popular at the end. Gothic **pinnacles** preceded the main trend and are a particularly noteworthy feature of certain Scottish churches built as early as the 1790s. This double revival of medieval styles would not affect churches only, but buildings of all sorts including country houses like Glassel in Kincardineshire, whose east wing in a Neo-Romanesque style was added in 1902.

Churches from the fifteenth century, in particular, are further discussed in section 4–7 below.

2–2
Style 1540–1660: Baronial glory days and the overthrow of the Church

The ephemeral character of smaller buildings that had characterised the pre-1540 period persisted into the next. Glen Shee, Glengairn and hundreds of other places throughout the Highlands and uplands are dotted with the remains of buildings that were held up by little more than good design and the occupants' willpower. But such structures existed in built-up areas also – the difference being that in towns, even the foundations have since been swept away. Most roofs in the period 1540–1660 were still of straw thatch, sometimes impregnated with clay; heather thatch; or in the humblest dwellings, cut turf. Manses (the middle-sized houses provided to parish ministers by the Church) were more often than not built of wattle and daub – sometimes known in Scotland as 'stake and rice', 'stud and mud', or 'clout and clay'. Such houses, one inhabitant noted, could 'not defend wind and rain'[8] and had to be rebuilt from scratch every twenty to thirty years. **Larbert Old Manse**

Larbert Old Manse

in Stirlingshire, from 1635, was by some stroke of luck built with walls of mortared stone (not clay) and with a tile roof (not thatch), and it is therefore one of just a handful of clues to the appearance of other ministers' houses of the time, not to mention other medium-sized, unfortified rural houses. Another, less 'pure' example is the Old Manse of Anstruther Easter, built in 1590–91 and extended in the following century.

The difference in cost between the various available modes of construction was immense. In Kincardineshire, a small mortared-stone house with a slate or wood roof was three to twelve times more expensive to build than a house of the same size held together with clay and roofed in thatch. In some areas, mud houses were made collectively by up to thirty men and women, over the course of a single day. Known as 'daubings', these festive events were the Scottish equivalent of the 'barn-raisings' of North America and may have helped inspire them.

The richer the owner, the sooner a slate roof was applied; and since 1920, roofs of perishable materials have scarcely been seen except in remote rural areas (see section 4–4, below). Original tile roofs from before 1660 will still be encountered, but mostly in coastal places with a history of trading with the Netherlands and Denmark;[9] the odd terra-cotta roof in a remote inland village probably indicates that the building once contained a smithy or some other highly flammable business operation. A door on an upper floor, accessed by a flight of external stone steps running parallel to the wall, is the main other 'tell' that a building of 1540–1660 was a workshop or storehouse. Well-preserved examples of this include the salmon-smoking facility known as **the 'Fish Hoose' near Peterhead**, Aberdeen-shire (1585); the very similar pistol factory in Doune, Stir-lingshire (1646); and the so-called King's Barn at Limekilns, Fife (sixteenth century). Rock Cottage, Joppa Pans (1635)

The 'Fish Hoose'
near Peterhead

was probably another example, though it has been altered almost beyond recognition; and the Pease Mill in Cockburnspath may be another. External steps were adopted in many such cases because of 'stone vaulted ground floors through which an internal staircase could not readily be made to pass'.[10]

In urban areas in this period, external arcades were introduced on some merchants' houses (for instance, Provost Ross's House in New Aberdeen, begun 1593) and a few major public buildings, including **Heriot's Hospital in Edinburgh** (1628–42) and the beautiful, now-demolished 1630–62 buildings of the University of Glasgow. However, **it was in the city of Elgin that arcades were most popular** and many can still be seen there. Surprisingly, in light of their apparent suitability for our rainy, windy climate, arcades have seldom been built here since the reign of Queen Anne (1702–14).[11] It is possible that their popularity declined because by the mid eighteenth century, goods were mostly sold in purpose-built shops rather than stored in merchants' own homes and dragged or rolled to the centre of town to be sold in the open air, as before. That being said, many

Right.
Heriot's Hospital
in Edinburgh

Opposite top.
Elgin arcades

Opposite bottom.
A 6-foot-high door
and 8-foot pend in
a late-16th-century
house in Banff

pre-1840 urban merchants' houses can be recognised by
the presence of a **pend**: essentially a ground-floor tunnel
connecting the back garden to the street. These are usually
off-centre to the house, and shallowly arched. Though
often thought to be driveways for carriages, many are too
low for this, while remaining wide enough for wheelbar-
rows, rolled barrels and so forth.

Mercat crosses

Above left.
Mercat Cross,
Langholm

Above right.
Airth Mercat
Cross

Opposite left.
New Aberdeen
Mercat Cross

Opposite right.
Prestonpans
Mercat Cross

In medieval and early modern Scots law, the right to trade in goods had to be positively conferred by the Crown, and in practice it was only granted to the inhabitants of certain towns and villages. Mercat i.e. market crosses served two purposes: first, to commemorate the granting of trading rights to a particular town; and secondly, to mark the exact spot at which trade was supposed to occur (retail shops had not yet come into being). Mercat crosses were also places of public proclamation, execution and corporal punishment.

At least since the Reformation of the Church in 1560, most have borne national symbols – especially the heraldic unicorn – rather than any overtly Christian imagery. At all times, however, their dominant feature was a tall stone post. According to the size and wealth of the community, this might merely be stuck into the

ground, as at Langholm and Banchory St Ternan; or be supported
on two to eight stone steps, as at Airth, Stirling, Dundee, Old
Aberdeen and Culross; or stand atop a small but often
elaborately decorated one-storey stone structure.

These 'cross-houses' might be round, oval, hexagonal,
octagonal or square. Some are just a solid block of masonry, as at
Kirkcudbright and Musselburgh. Others could incorporate an
arcade for traders' booths, as at New Aberdeen; or a very small
gaol, as at Prestonpans, Elgin and Fraserburgh. Most mercat
crosses have been moved or altered in some way, but a surprising
percentage still exist in some form (including war memorials).
Post-1840 replacement crosses can often be recognised by their
use of a purely decorative, Neo-Gothic style: for instance at
Forres (1844) and Turriff (1865).

The towers of the rural gentry became significantly more embellished in the 1540–1660 period, with Craigievar in Aberdeenshire (completed 1626) being perhaps the world's best-loved example. With regard to towers in particular, the period saw: 1) 'a general increase in the size of window openings, and the more frequent use of glass'; 2) greater – albeit far from perfect – symmetry in the placement of windows and their size; and 3) the disappearance of defensive parapet walkways.[12] This was also the period of, if not the arrival, then a more intensive use of turrets and other similar features described in section 4–8, below. As with palaces in the preceding period, much of this new embellishment can be ascribed to French influence. However, it is inescapable that in terms of 'footprint', overall size, width-to-height ratio, and roof-angles, the typical small Scottish castle of 1540–1660 is more like the typical Danish manor-house of the same era than it is like anything else; the main difference being that the Danish ones were constructed of brick and had tile roofs.

Key points of style for Scottish buildings of 1540–1660, urban and rural, noble and ordinary, include: short doorways, often of less than seven feet; most ceilings correspondingly low; small windows, usually of less than three feet on any side, except in large public buildings; **steep rooflines**, i.e. with the angle of the peak as small as 60 degrees, and almost always less than 90 degrees; and dormer windows that are not set back from the main wall, but rise directly out of it, with only the upper part of the window in the dormer proper and the lower part in the main wall (see section 4–9, below). **Musselburgh High Street** (opposite) clearly illustrates the typical size-, roofline-, and window-arrangement discrepancies between urban houses of *c.* 1840 (left), *c.* 1770 (middle) and *c.* 1630 (right). The dormers of the seventeenth-century house in the picture are especially ornate for a townhouse, probably because

Top.
The 16th-century
manse of Dunlop,
showing the
period's typical
'cat-slide' dormers
and roof-peak
angle of around
60 degrees

Left.
Musselburgh High
Street

this one belonged to the French ambassador. But even the
townhouses of great noblemen, for example the Earl
Marischal's 1599 dwelling in Port Henry Lane, Peterhead
(illus. in my book *Lost Banff and Buchan*, p. 124), sometimes featured unadorned 'cat-slide' dormers that would

also have been seen on farmhouses, ministers' manses and merchants' houses of the same period.

'Retro' copying of the more ornate, triangle-topped dormers from this period began in the 1840s and was especially popular from 1890 to 1930. However, copying of the plainer, 'cat-slide' dormer was fairly rare until after the Second World War in most areas. So as of the time of writing, at least, the presence of 'cat-slides' on a building that is not blatantly new is a strong indication that it is from before 1660. Conversely, ornate dormers sometimes show up on humbler buildings: for instance, the 1680s **Quaker school in Kinmuck, Aberdeenshire**. It should be stressed, however, that dormers that do *not* join up with a main wall, i.e. that rise directly out of the roofing material on all sides, could have been added at almost any time, and their diagnostic value is therefore very small.

Quaker School in Kinmuck, Aberdeenshire

Dormers

The main difference between wall-head dormers of the pre-1660 and post-1840 periods is in the width of the masonry surrounding the window itself. The originals (top right and bottom left) typically have surrounds of not more than one foot in width. Later homages (top left) tend to have margins of fifteen inches or more, with the windows themselves often being larger as well. This is not an absolute rule, however. 'Retro' dormers – especially from after 1920 – can be as small as, and have edges as thin as, the pre-1660 originals.

Top left.
Fat-sided retro dormers

Top right.
Kilravock Castle detail

Above left.
Rose and Fleur-de-lys topped wallhead dormers, early 17th century

Above right.
Bay-fronted dormers originated in the Victorian period and have been made ever since. These are originals of c.1880

Typical features: early seventeenth century

The House of Dudwick painted by James Giles RSA (1801–70)

By being demolished soon after this picture was painted, the House of Dudwick (1636) escaped the dominant Victorian trend of piling 'Baronial' touches on to buildings of all sorts – including even houses built by barons. Key features to note, all typical of early-seventeenth-century houses of the merchants and lesser nobility, are: 1) the square or nearly square chimneys with plain, but pronounced mouldings around the tops; 2) roof-angles of somewhat less than 90 degrees; 3) dormer windows (in this case with 'cat-slides') that break upward through the wall-head; 4) windows that are not centred, relative either to the centre of the wall they are in, or to one another; and 5) a small semi-circular tower, probably built to accommodate a spiral staircase. The doorway at centre right, judging by its height and integral window, will be from after 1750 – whether an improvement of a smaller, windowless original doorway, or new altogether. The part-thatched one-storey building at the far right, on the evidence of its enormous (but still square) chimney, could have contained a bakery or forge.

Though the period 1540–1660 has been generally regarded – not least by its Victorian copyists – as the 'most Scottish' period of Scottish architecture, numerous foreign influences can be traced. Scotland was formally allied with France up to 1560 in law, and perhaps even longer in spirit.[13] Anna of Denmark was our queen from 1589 to 1619, and Heriot's Hospital (illus. p. 24) has been explicitly compared to Frederiksborg Palace in Hillerød, Denmark; while the convergent style of Scottish tower-houses and Danish manor-houses in this period has already been noted above. Perhaps most significantly, much of the Scottish higher nobility decamped to London in 1603 with King James VI, who was concurrently King James I of England from that year until his death in 1625. There, king and courtiers were exposed not only to 'home-grown' English architecture, but English interpretations of Italian architecture.

2–3
Style 1660–1750: de-fortification, symmetry and the emergence of architecture as a profession

Many architectural historians (and historical signposts) take the Reformation of the Scottish Church in 1560 as an absolute turning point, before which buildings were 'medieval' – and after which, presumably, they were 'modern'. But this is true only of churches, and only some churches at that. In every part of the realm, numerous buildings that had been built for Catholic worship continued in use by the new state Church, sometimes until they literally fell apart. Instead, the really profound watershed in Scottish and British architecture, and culture generally, was formed by the Civil Wars and Puritan dictatorships of 1638–60. The generation that waged these wars tended to be fundamentalist in their views, whatever these happened to be. They did not yet take the Grand Tour of the Continent, and their foreign business interests did not inevitably lead them to go abroad either. Largely uninterested in science, engineering and technology, they would scarcely have recognised the concept of the professional architect, and were content to use furniture, rooms and buildings little different from those of the 1400s. The motive force of our post-1660 culture, on the other hand, was the host of younger, cultured people who, having been ruined by the wars or persecuted by the repressive wartime regimes, were driven abroad – largely to France, Holland and Scandinavia. These included King Charles II, who, having been crowned at Scone in January 1651, aged twenty, spent most of the next decade in exile in Bruges, Brussels, Paris and Cologne. His generation came home to roost in 1660, full of new architectural ideas, and found a war-ravaged and neglected country to rebuild.

This is not to suggest that the 1640s and 1650s produced nothing of value in architecture; just nothing that would allow us to stand up and shout, Eureka! This was the moment, the person, the building, that changed everything. The effects of Oliver Cromwell's occupation of Scotland were chiefly subtractive. Medieval St Machar's Cathedral in Old Aberdeen was half-wrecked as a source of building stone for artillery fortifications; Ardchattan Priory was burned; the old Castle of Rosslyn was destroyed by cannon fire and the famous Rosslyn Chapel (1440–70) used as a stable; 4,300 Scots were killed on the battlefield at Dunbar, or allowed to starve as prisoners afterwards; and the town of Dundee was sacked, with a thousand men, women and children put to the sword. Some interesting architectural additions were made to Scotland's ancient universities in the 1650s – in at least two cases, thanks to pious Cromwellian officers' money. But broadly speaking, this deeply

St Machar's
Cathedral, Aberdeen

unpleasant and unproductive era pressed the reset button
on our entire culture in a way that the Reformation had
not. The seventy-five years between the first delivery of
private letters by the post office in 1637 and the invention
of the piano in 1709 were marked by a fever of (now seemingly mundane) innovation. In addition to sash windows
(see section 4–10), the fork, the banknote, the cheque,
upholstery, female actors, watches, table-clocks, the barom-
eter, Father Christmas, a standing army equipped principally
with firearms, French cookery books, firemen, 'classical'

35

music, professional horse racing, machine-made coinage, coffee, tea, china cups, gin, port, chocolate, opera and cricket all first gained wide acceptance in Britain, or were invented, during this stunningly short time. Moreover, these innovations are disproportionately *still* in widespread use, by a present-day populace that has abandoned the steam engine, telegraph, phonograph and paddle-wheel, and is on the verge of abandoning the typewriter, film, terrestrial broadcasting and perhaps even telephony in favour of silicon-based equivalents. In architecture, the effects of this seventeenth-century sea-change can be perceived in buildings of every type: urban and rural, communal and private, good, bad and indifferent.

Prior to and during the Civil Wars, architectural design was the preserve of the secretive and more-or-less hereditary medieval craft of masonry, embodied by the three generations of the Mylne family who dominated major public building projects in Scotland from 1615 to 1671, and the Bel family who built some of the finest castles in the northeast of Scotland from the 1560s to the 1630s. William Schaw, as well as being Master of the King's Works in Scotland from 1583 until his death in 1602, is widely claimed as a founder of freemasonry – though just how far *free*masonry differed from actual building work prior to the eighteenth century remains an open question. William Wallace,[14] deacon of the Edinburgh Masons' Lodge, was Master Mason to James VI and then Charles I from 1617 until his death. He has sometimes been given credit for the design of **Pinkie House**, one of the grandest private residences of the Jacobean age – though typically, there is no firm proof of his involvement.

The pivotal figure in the transition from master masons to professional architects was Wallace's pupil William Aitoun, a Haddington man who succeeded Wallace as King's Master Mason in 1631. Aitoun was responsible for

Pinkie House

successfully completing one of the most magnificent buildings Edinburgh has ever seen, Heriot's Hospital (1628–42;
illus. p. 24), and for **Innes House** in Morayshire (1641–
53; illus. p. 38): the only grand Scottish country mansion
to be conceived and built entirely within the Civil War
period. On the evidence of style alone, Aitoun may also
have had a hand in the remarkable 1634 palace wing of
Caerlaverock Castle. For designing Innes House, he was
paid £26 13s 4d Scots (about £4,900 today). But in keeping

Innes House

Caerlaverock
Castle

with his Masonic tradition he was a self-effacing man who left few records, and for two centuries after Aitoun's death, the credit for nearly all of his work was routinely assigned – on no evidence at all – to the more famous Welsh designer, Inigo Jones (1573–1652). Like so much else, the emergence of architecture as a profession, not dominated by guilds, family dynasties or secret societies, would await the 1660 restoration of the monarchy.

The once-exiled King Charles II perhaps naturally chose persons with similar experiences of Continental travel for important posts. In 1671 he appointed Capt. John Slezer (d. 1717), a German, as his Chief Engineer in Scotland. Beginning in 1678, Slezer made a series of detailed drawings of Scotland's towns. In addition to being very useful guides to prevailing Scottish building styles of the late seventeenth century, the resulting book[15] has been called the first work that 'aimed to depict an entire country'.[16] Even more significantly to our story, the king appointed Sir William Bruce as Surveyor-General of the King's Works in Scotland, in the same year that Slezer became Chief Engineer. Bruce was a Fife-born Episcopalian who had sat out the Cromwell years as a merchant in the Netherlands. Robert Mylne, third-generation Master Mason to the Crown, was retained, but was placed in a subordinate position, largely following Bruce's orders after 1671; and if the architectural profession in Scotland has a start date, this was probably it.

The undoubtedly tense but long-running Bruce/Mylne collaboration began a slow process by which members of Bruce's circle and their Scottish students and imitators would dominate not merely Scottish architecture, but British architecture as a whole, for more than a hundred years.[17] James Smith (d. 1731), from Tarbat in Ross-shire, worked under Bruce and Mylne on the 1670s rebuilding of Holyrood Palace, and took over Bruce's post in 1683, going on to collaborate with Mylne (by this time his father-in-law)

Buildings in late-
17th-century
Edinburgh,
sketched by
Capt. John Slezer

on the splendid 120-room 'pink palace' of Drumlanrig Castle. Smith produced his own highly advanced plans for the **Kirk of the Canongate** (1688–90), as well as the David Crawford townhouse in Hamilton (1696; now the Cameronians Museum) and many other splendid buildings. Smith taught his principles to Colen Campbell, who was born in Brodie Castle near Forres in 1676. Campbell toured Italy for seven years before returning to Scotland in 1702 to set up as an architect and influential architectural writer. His writing is sometimes credited with preventing the Baroque

Canongate Kirk, Edinburgh

style (see section 4–7) from taking hold in Britain, despite its having powerful champions in Englishmen Sir Christopher Wren and Sir John Vanbrugh – and despite the fact that Campbell's own designs influenced Castle Howard in Yorkshire, the grandest Baroque residence ever built in the British Isles. However, aside from the magnificent **Shawfield Mansion** in Glasgow (1711), Campbell did little in his native Scotland, and his dozens of commissions are mostly south of the border.[18]

Campbell's great rival, James Gibbs, had a very different

Shawfield
Mansion

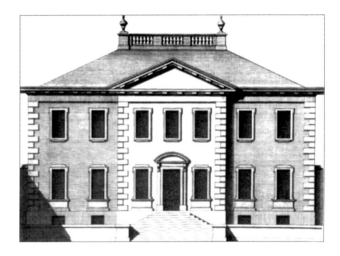

background (lower middle class, Catholic and Tory) but a surprisingly similar career path. Born in the ramshackle fishing village of Footdee, Aberdeen in 1682, Gibbs studied in Rome, as well as in London under Wren. Many would agree that he outstripped his master, and that most of the best 'Wren' parish churches are actually by Gibbs, whose solo work includes St Martin-in-the-Fields and St Mary-le-Strand. In contrast to Campbell, who at least produced Shawfield, Gibbs seems to have done no work in Scotland at all – much of the slack being taken up by Fife-born William Adam (1689–1748). But this is not to say that Gibbs's influence was not felt in Scotland. The Campbell/Gibbs rivalry was a highly dynamic one, and some would say that 'Georgian style' itself (see section 3–3) was the result.

Though he is not known to have ever worked south of Carlisle himself, William Adam has been criticised as a mere copyist of the ideas of the English-based Scot, Gibbs; and more cruelly, perhaps, as someone who only had a career at all because by 1720 James Smith was too old to continue working. Yet, the tradition of Scottish success in British architecture – arguably amounting to domination – would be continued by William Adam's sons, John (1721– 92), Robert (1728–92) and James (1732–94), and by Sir William Chambers (1723–96), who was born to Scottish parents in Sweden. James Adam succeeded his brother Robert as Architect of the King's Works in 1768, by which time the latter was 'the most sought-after architect in Britain'.[19]

In hindsight, it can be seen that the Civil War period's unique combination of opportunities and novel ideas for rebuilding had started a small avalanche: leading in the end to a national, British architecture that happened to be dominated by men of Scottish birth. Honourably, William Adam set his face against this trend, calling for a distinctively Scottish architecture (and implicitly critiquing the pan-British pretensions of Campbell's work); and yet, Adam's **Craigdarroch House, built in Dumfriesshire in 1729**, can seem today to be simply an English Queen Anne house that happens not to be made of brick.

Even before Sir William Bruce first set pen to paper as

Craigdarroch House

an architect in the 1670s, however, the scene was changing. The immediate post-1660 years exhibited a hope, amounting almost to an expectation, that major civil unrest would never recur. Exterior walls became thinner; doors lost their protective iron grilles; windows grew larger and more numerous; gun-ports ceased to be installed; vulnerable thatched roofs came nearer to the ground. Gone was the need to see (and shoot) out of a house in every conceivable direction, so floor-plans became simple rectangles. This simplicity of ground plan was joined by the flatter surfaces and increasingly symmetrical door- and window arrangements popularly associated with the Georgian period (1714–1830). It was also in the 1660–1750 period that the higher

Castles no more

Left.
Ardgrain

Right.
Balnacraig

Scotland's first true country houses, perfectly symmetrical and almost totally unfortified, were built by successful townsmen who set themselves up as country gentlemen after the Restoration. They are, in some sense, free-standing versions of the town-houses of the immediate pre-Civil War period. These examples are Nether Ardgrain (1664) and Balnacraig (1673).

social classes in urban areas began to favour high-set front doors accessed by a step, or even a whole flight of steps as at Shawfield, illustrated on p. 42.

In some ways, the grander buildings of 1660–1750 were a grassroots, 'Chinese whispers' interpretation of the buildings of ancient Greece and Rome, via the designs of Italian architect Andrea Palladio (1508–80) and Welsh architect Inigo Jones, and/or the owners' personal experiences of Continental or Scandinavian exile. Sir William Bruce and his Scottish colleagues and successors merely picked up on this grassroots tendency, elevated it into a set of formal principles, and successfully re-exported it to the richer and more populous southern kingdom. Moreover, as Britons

Shopping moves indoors

Before the period 1660–1750, when retail shops of a very general kind made their first widespread appearance, commerce was carried on almost exclusively in the open air: at street markets (usually around market crosses), country fairs and quays. Toward the end of the period, shops specialising in a particular type of commodity appeared. Throughout the country, from Haddington (pictured) to Biggar and Aberdeen to the Isle of Mull, the larger examples of these new retail establishments of the eighteenth century were built to a particular pattern: usually with a four-window frontage and a central, street-facing third gable. This middle gable might or might not have a chimney, but usually had a width of two windows, as shown. It was only after 1840, however, that retail premises eclipsed fairs and street markets altogether.

Hiding in plain sight

Never let garish paint, lurid signage, satellite dishes and horrible plastic windows distract you from a building's 'lines'. Sandwiched between block of flats built in 1900 (left) and a commercial building from 1845 (right), this Chinese restaurant suggests – by its short stature, small windows, steep roofline, and cherub-decorated double wall sundial – a building of a much earlier era. With regard to stature in particular, its left-hand doorway has no step down to the pavement and is only 6.5 feet in height. Subject to further investigation, a construction date in the period 1720–50

seems likely. Library research reveals that it was already a commercial building in 1903 (Stephen Forrest China and Glass Merchant); and this fact, coupled with its asymmetrical window arrangement and multiple front doors, suggest that it could have been purpose-built as a retail shop. If so, it would be one of the oldest in the country. However, it could equally well have been a rather unexceptional small inn.

increasingly directed their warlike energy against France rather than against each other, many fewer people ended up in exile in Holland, France and Scandinavia. So the eighteenth century saw these particular foreign influences erode; and despite the supplanting of Britain's native royal family by German cousins in 1714, German influences on building styles were negligible. A high-end, theoretical interest in Italian architecture filled the vacuum, but only partially. Architecturally, Great Britain was becoming more united – and more isolated – than ever before.

2–4
Style 1750–1840: Pan-British Neo-Classical style consolidated, amid increasing scale and the first stirrings of 'retro'

The famous 'Age of Improvement' in Scottish agriculture coincided with a step-change in the scale of buildings. Farmhouses, as a category of structure, were fairly rare before this period: landowners mostly lived in mansions or castles, while poorer rural people inhabited small, self-sufficient and more or less disposable hamlets (known as clachans or fermtouns), consisting of five or ten single-storey cottages of unmortared fieldstone. So, if few farmhouses from before 1750 can now be found, it is in part because the figure of the prosperous Scottish family farmer of a few hundred acres, not himself a nobleman, is essentially a post-1750 concept, except in the Borders. It was in this period, then, that the normal Scots farmhouse of two storeys and a width of three windows came to be built in really large numbers. Nevertheless, demand outstripped supply, and many pre-1750 unfortified laird's mansions, including Dudwick (p. 32) and Ardgrain (p. 44), passed into use as farmhouses at this time.

It was also in this period that numerous clachans were cleared of their inhabitants, either to be consolidated into single-family farms, or to fall into utter decay. The creation of new planned villages also reached a peak. Scotland had always been remarkably different from England in this area: from 1500 to 1641, for example, when the English founded no new towns at all (except in their colonies in the western hemisphere), the Scots created at least 150, doubling the number that had previously existed. More than a hundred more were founded on 'greenfield' sites or drained swamps between 1677 and 1839. After 1840, industrial production and other sources of employment shifted from the countryside to the cities, bringing the new-village movement to an end, for the time being. But visitors from countries such as France, England and Belgium – whose first ages of prosperity were centuries earlier, and much more prosperous, than Scotland's – can be surprised by the almost raw newness of most Scottish village architecture in comparison to their own.

Amid all these complex developments in Scottish society, the main change in architecture was not so much of style but scale. The typical Scottish house from 1800 is 30 per cent taller per floor than a house from 1700 built for the same sort of person. Windows and doorways grew in proportion. So that doors themselves did not grow impractically large and unwieldy, the exterior doorways of 1750–1840 increasingly saw **transom windows** set into them directly above the door (see also section 4–11). Other stylistic changes also occurred, of course. Harling fell out of favour quite rapidly, particularly among the elite, to be replaced by a much higher grade of stonework than had previously been used on buildings that were harled. Not

Rectangular transom window of c. 1800

only the surfaces of the stones, but their edges, became more regular; so did their colours, relative to one another. So while Scottish buildings of the 1750–1840 era would never achieve the 'wedding cake' appearance of the fully-plastered brick houses of, say, Earl's Court, it is remarkable how close they came to this look using stone alone.

It might be supposed that the new-town phenomenon that characterised Scotland's development continually from the Middle Ages to 1840 was a form of speculative building. In fact, it usually consisted of little more than a declaration that a town (with a legal right to engage in trade) now existed on a particular site. Empty lots were then leased or sold, and the new inhabitants built their houses – and latterly shops – at their own expense. True speculative building was therefore a new phenomenon in the 1750–1840 period, though its customers were as yet limited to the urban elite (see section 3–5). It was as a by-product of this new phenomenon of speculative building for the well-off that the country's first semi-detached and terraced houses were built: the **first semis** appearing in Thistle Court, Edinburgh in 1767.[20]

Prior to 1750, most external ironwork was of a theoretically defensive character, e.g. grilles protecting doors (known as 'yetts') and the large gates that guarded lairds' houses, both in the countryside and in towns. But the 1750–1840 period, when the advent of industrial production made worked metal more readily available, became the heyday of decorative external ironwork, especially in the larger towns. Typically, this consisted of railings to protect passersby from falling into 'areas' (i.e. wells/steps down to

Thistle Court

front entrances to the basement) or to prevent them treading on the flowers – front 'areas' and urban front gardens both being new developments of this period also. In addition to railings, many fine houses of 1800–40 boasted their own small iron lamp-posts of ostensibly Ancient Greek appearance. Implausibly tiny iron balconies likewise became fashionable.

Urban elegance: early nineteenth century

A railed-in 'area', in this case with an integral lamp-post; door-sized windows; and a bridge over the 'area' to a front door featuring a transom window – in this case a 'fanlight' because of its fan shape – are all typical features of grand urban houses from 1800–40. However, the deeply grooved, 'rusticated' blocks making up the ground floor are not a *period* feature, insofar as they were used on a minority of expensive buildings from the late seventeenth century until after the First World War, more or less without interruption.

It should be mentioned that iron railings used to be far more numerous; most were collected in 1940, ostensibly to be melted down for use in munitions, and only those deemed 'of artistic merit' were allowed to survive. Thus, the old railings (considered as a group) were presumably much plainer than those which remain. Nevertheless, the survivors exhibit a charming array of shapes ranging from roses, thistles and tulips to swords, halberds and spears. One can also frequently observe long rows of small metal squares in a now-purposeless line of masonry on the ground, where railings have been sawn off. Whole cast-iron shop-fronts (often featuring a design of narrow classical columns) were also erected beginning in the 1750–1840 period, in villages as well as the major towns, and these have had a better survival rate.

This period, when Scotland was officially referred to as 'North Britain' in most government documents, also saw the firm consolidation – particularly in the cities – of the pan-British architectural style that had been pioneered by expatriate Scots of previous generations. By 1801, indeed, we can find few differences (other than the choice of locally-produced building materials) between the fashionable town-houses of Edinburgh, Dublin, Bath and other cities of the newly united UK. It is noteworthy that even the *end* of this stylistic consensus was brought about by a London-trained Scot: William Burn (1789–1870), whose virtuoso ability to design great-looking buildings in the Neo-Classical, 'mock-castle', French Gothic, English Perpendicular and Scottish Baronial styles made him one of the most sought-after architects of the late Georgian era – in Ireland and England as much as in Scotland. Burn's talent and success made 'retro' seem plausible to architectural patrons; and if there is one person who can be said to have caused the major sea-change in Scottish architecture around 1840, Burn is the man. Only in the second quarter of the nineteenth century, with the sudden and slightly shocking appearance of retro-Baronialism – particularly driven by Burn, and by novelist/national huckster Sir Walter Scott – would a distinctively Scottish architectural scene re-emerge; and not always to the best effect.[21]

The Georgian Neo-Gothic or 'mock-castle' style, despite its rise and fall having occurred entirely within this period, was never dominant within it.[22] As such, it is discussed in detail under 'Battlements and crenellations', section 4–3 below.

2–5
Style 1840–1920: 'retro', diversity, mechanisation and unparalleled prosperity

After 1840, the Scottish architectural scene changed almost as dramatically as it had after 1660, but in different ways and for different reasons. Britain's first empire, in North America, had been continually threatened by the French and various sections of its own inhabitants, and had been run at a steep financial loss. But her second, in India, was vastly profitable. Scottish people of all classes were now able to improve their financial position through direct or indirect participation in imperial trade and administration. As the treasure of Asia poured in, Scotland experienced a rebuilding boom even more profound than that of the post-Civil War period. Houses of all sorts became even bigger. Retail shops – themselves a radical (but now seemingly mundane) invention of 1660–1750 – became larger, more numerous and more specialised. But money was not the only factor. Whole towns expanded as trains, and eventually trams and motorcars, abetted suburbanisation. Soon suburban villas, each of them far more spacious than the average nobleman's house of 1700, sat cheek by jowl on sites that had been green fields a few years before. Likewise, minor public and commercial buildings such as schools, banks and workshops – all of which had been, as of the mid eighteenth century, hardly distinguishable from large single-family dwellings – grew to the size of palaces.

The numbers and types of churches had multiplied steadily between 1790 and 1860 as the bold religious liberalisation policies of King George III, and later of Prime Minister the Duke of Wellington, broke the stranglehold of the Establishment. As Catholicism grew more respectable, Neo-Gothic nods to the cathedrals of the Middle Ages began to supersede the Neo-Classical (i.e. Roman/pagan) style that had prevailed during the late eighteenth century's Age of Reason.

The English Arts and Crafts movement, a voluble intellectual outcry that was for Neo-Gothic and against Neo-Classical architecture,[23] was heard loud and clear north of the border. In Glasgow, suddenly home to Scotland's highest number and highest proportion of Catholics, even the Baroque style was dramatically revived. Episcopal churches and chapels had been a quiet presence in Scotland since the seventeenth century; but these also multiplied as railway-equipped Scotland became, for the first time, a mass tourist destination for English people – as well as a place for the English (and Irish, and Colonial) elite to shoot and fish, send their children to school, and in some cases to put down roots. Scottish slums grew exponentially, as dismissed or disgruntled rural workers sought better conditions, sometimes in vain, in the cities. And the more prosperous members of the working class began to buy their own homes. All these changes had one thing in common: the demand they created for new structures was enormous, and 10–20 per cent of all Scottish buildings now standing date from the period 1840–1920 alone.

Under this pressure, traditional building styles that had

evolved slowly over generations gave way to a book-learned architectural internationalism, and its mirror image: book-learned reactive Scottish nationalism.[24] Soon, ranks of 'Scottish Baronial', 'French Gothic', and 'Tudor' mansions, all brand new, could glower at each other across nine feet of lawn, as their stiff-collared inhabitants dreamed or fretted about far bigger lawns in far-off Colombo and Simla. But this is not to say that the later nineteenth century was without its architectural gems and wonders; and for sheer solidity – aided by the application of industrial methods to both quarrying and construction – the age has not been equalled since.

60 Princes Street, Edinburgh

The Georgian Neo-Gothic or 'mock-castle' movement of 1750–1840 (see section 4–3) had inaugurated the first great age of 'retro'. But it was the era after 1840 that embodied it fully, and saw many – or perhaps most – new Scottish buildings erected in a multitude of styles copied from previous eras and/or other nations. The Tudor, Elizabethan and Jacobean styles, all of which arose in England between c. 1450 and 1625, became popular again throughout the period 1840–1920, not only in Scotland (which was never ruled by the Tudors) but across Britain and the British Empire. In addition to whole buildings built in these styles, notably **60 Princes Street, Edinburgh** (1903), houses and shops incorporated bits and pieces of each of them, such as exposed wood on gables and dormers – particularly in the 1890s.[25]

External woodwork returns

Two main types of Victorian and Edwardian Scottish gable- and dormer woodwork. Along with pairs and/or trios of identically-sized windows, this exposed woodwork is often your first and best clue that a building dates from 1880 to 1910.

It would, however, be a mistake to chalk this up entirely to English 'cultural imperialism', since half-timbered buildings were commonplace in Scotland in the fifteenth and sixteenth centuries, while the 'Jacob' whose name is referenced in the term Jacobean style (King James VI and I) was a Scot who ruled both countries.[26] However, it can feel like an English import, because few if indeed any genuine Scottish half-timbered structures survived our rebuilding booms of 1660–1840 and the not unrelated 'Age of Improvement' in agriculture. Tourist-trail water-muddying plays its usual role here. The staff of the Huntly Arms Hotel in Aboyne, Aberdeenshire are justifiably proud that their establishment has been open since the 1400s; but not one bit of what remains of the building is from before 1770, and various additions and revisions have made it, in effect, a Victorian retro-Jacobean structure.

As we have seen, whether in the countryside or in towns, the houses of Scotland's nobility in the period 1540–1660 were generally *not* half-timbered, but built almost entirely of stone. Another characteristic of 1840–1920 Scottish building is the application of superficial features of these nobles' houses to government buildings, hotels, shops and the houses of the middle classes. It is not uncommon to see even arrow-slits in Scottish suburbia, and I have heard at least one architectural expert speaking dismissively of the 'railway-hotel Baronial style'. Perhaps feeling under pressure from the perceived Englishness of Victorian neo-Tudor buildings, a number of Scots architects working in this period tried to isolate and replicate the truly Scottish features of sixteenth-century buildings – without, it must be noted, questioning the rage for 'retro' that totally dominated their own time, in the spheres of furniture and interior design as much as in exterior architecture.[27] Couched as history, and still incredibly useful to historians and tourists alike, the books published in this period by David MacGibbon, Thomas Ross, R.W. Billings and James Gillespie[28] were nevertheless part of an agenda regarding *new* buildings of their own time.

Few Victorian retro buildings are able to fool us for very long. All or nearly all of their proportions are 'off'. The tower of the current Balmoral Castle, which replaced a genuine sixteenth-century tower-house in 1855, is too tall by half; **Donaldson's College in Edinburgh**, built in a *c.* 1600 style by W.H. Playfair in 1851, is too big all over; and everywhere, doors and windows are too tall, window-panes too broad. On the far reaches of cities, where suburbia gives way to actual countryside, houses gravitate to a partic-ular size: too short and squat to be a genuine tower-house, despite being a compendium of oversized parts. This is to say nothing of the fact that purpose-built police stations (to take just one category of example) did not exist before

the Victorian period at all; Edinburgh's **Portobello Police Station**, built as such in 1878, is an uneasy mixture of sixteenth-century Scots and nineteenth-century French features. By and large, the Victorians – unlike the predecessors they imitated – followed the dictates of Anglo-French Arts and Crafts forerunner A.W.N. Pugin (1812–52): that a building should be designed 'from the inside out': i.e. with the inhabitants' convenience taking precedence over exterior appearances.[29] The bay window (section 4–16), which adds interior space and light but is usually destructive of exterior symmetry, is an important practical expression of the Victorian 'inside first' philosophy. This philosophy collided head-on with, and frequently sank, the era's inevitably superficial schemes of 'retro' exterior styling. And it is this exterior wrongness, taken as a whole, that some people unconsciously mean when they speak

Donaldson's College, Edinburgh

Portobello Police Station

dismissively of a 'Victorian style'. Nor did the Victorians ever question the disappearance of harling after 1750 or make any serious efforts to revive it. On the contrary, they rejected not only harling, but also the smooth, even masonry that had replaced it during 1750–1840: experimenting instead with a wide variety of new surface treatments, including pseudo-random arrangements of masonry; bold colour schemes using contrasting colours of natural stone – often yellow and red; and eventually, mechanical techniques to 'distress' stones, in awkward mimicry of the 'rough-hewn' work of some largely imaginary olden time (see also section 4–19, below).

This barrage of 'retro', affecting everything from individual stones upwards, led Scotland largely to miss out on the 'smooth' and relatively forward-looking Art Nouveau style of 1883–c 1920. The first-ever piece of work in this style[30] was a book-cover designed by a presumably Scottish-descended London architect, A.H. Mackmurdo, who in the event did not design any Art Nouveau buildings. In interior design, which was considered an integral part of the movement, two of the style's three most important UK practitioners were Glasgow Scots: Margaret Macdonald (1864–1933) and her husband, Charles Rennie Mackintosh (1868–1928),[31] who like Mackmurdo also designed exteriors. Nevertheless, Mackintosh was so clearly inspired by Japanese design – subject of a powerful craze in Britain following the defeat of our greatest post-Waterloo enemy, imperial Russia, by our close ally imperial Japan in 1905

58

Charles Rennie Macintosh designed the House for an Art Lover (right) and Glasgow School of Art (below), both forerunners of the Art Deco style

– that his buildings usually appear to be forerunners of Art Deco (see next section) rather than examples of Art Nouveau.

Oddly, alongside their passion for 'retro' styling, the Victorians exhibited a stronger than usual urge to modernise and improve everything they came across. Thus, a major pitfall in reading Scottish buildings is that almost any typical feature of Victorian-era architecture could have been retro-fitted to a building of any earlier period. Bay windows, in particular, were applied to buildings of all ages in the nine-teenth and early twentieth centuries, while dormers (except those that join up with the wall-head) are so likely to be later additions that you are simply advised to ignore them altogether.

Bays aside, Scottish windows of 1840–1920 tended to be narrower relative to their height than those of prior eras, even if they were larger overall. Whether as a cause or an effect of this, window pairs, trios and bays went from curiosities at the beginning of the period to dominant styles at the end. These are discussed in depth in Chapter 4, below.

One feature that the Victorians appear actually to have invented is the '**kneeler**': a fairly long extension, into a hori-zontal direction, of an otherwise triangular dormer or gable. A structure that veers off horizontally in this way can itself be referred to as a 'kneeler gable' or 'kneeler dormer'. More often than not, the gable/dormer and 'kneelers' are 'knife-edged' on top as shown in our picture (opposite, top), though flat ones are known too. Perhaps because they are often so thin, it is also fairly rare for 'kneeler' gables to contain chimneys. They are more likely to terminate in a terracotta ball, an iron spike, or some other purely deco-rative flourish, where pre-1840 structures would tend to have either a chimney or nothing at all. Rival Scottish archi-tects William Burn and W.H. Playfair both used 'kneelers' extensively in the 1830s and '40s. But this feature does

Elaborate and simple examples of Victorian kneelers

not, to the best of my knowledge, have any earlier basis in the architecture of Scotland or indeed of any other country – unless it is as a grotesque exaggeration of the 'skewputts' of the seventeenth and eighteenth centuries (see p. 62). Given this late appearance, you should regard 'kneelers' as strong evidence of a post-1840 origin, at least for that part of the building; see also under 'the case of Lauriston Castle', section 3–6 below.

Skewputts

'Skewputts' are small but structurally important stones located where the wall-head, gable-end and roofing material all meet. This one is part of the crowstepped late-seventeenth-century customhouse of Crail in Fife, but non-crowstepped buildings also utilised them. Skewputts often carry dates of construction or other inscriptions that can be small and easy to miss. On very tall buildings, especially from before 1750, it may be worth examining the skewputts through binoculars.

Though individual architects of this period – including Burn, Burn's pupil David Bryce, Mackintosh, and Sir Robert Lorimer – were recognised for greatness in their lifetimes, most architectural work would henceforth largely be carried on by firms.

2–6
Style after 1920: 'retro' perfected, Art Deco, Brutalism and green architecture

After the death of Queen Victoria in 1901, the rage for 'retro' architecture that had characterised her sixty-five-year reign began to abate; but where it was still practised, it became considerably more accurate. The 1920s additions to Dunnottar Castle, for example, are notoriously difficult to spot, and **Broughton Place in Peeblesshire, built in 1936–37** to a design by India-born Scot Sir Basil Spence (1907–76), may be the most convincing mock tower house of all time – though others continue to be built. A further change,

Broughton Place,
Peeblesshire

which began just prior to the First World War, was that
Georgian as well as pre-Georgian designs became ripe for
copying: the former being popular enough to acquire its
own nickname, 'Neo-Geo'. This, too, is harder to detect
than any pre-1920 'retro' project. Fortunately, 'retro' in
the interwar years and since has been a rare and rarefied
pursuit. 'The masses', as they were now known, had other
fish to fry.

Elsewhere, including especially France, Catalonia, Austria-Hungary and the USA, a style called Art Nouveau had taken hold just before the First World War. But Scotland's very different architectural development – which missed out altogether the Rococo style that had been dominant on the Continent in the eighteenth century – had no historical basis from which Art Nouveau could emerge. And even its greatest supporter, Mackintosh, precociously adopted an Art Deco style for exteriors (see previous section), rendering Art Nouveau stillborn. In Scotland, its influence would be limited chiefly to small interior items such as chairs and picture frames.

Mackintosh died in 1928. His place in Scottish and British architecture was inherited by Spence, who is considerably less famous than Mackintosh today, despite having been more successful in his own lifetime. In addition to superior 'retro' structures like Broughton Place, Spence was a driving force behind both the beloved Art Deco style of the interwar years, and the postwar style decried as Brutalism, working not just in Scotland and England but throughout the Commonwealth.

The keynote of the Art Deco style, at least as practised in Scotland, is horizontality, equally affecting roofs (usually flat), windows ('landscape' format), and window-panes (also often 'landscape' format). This bold new combination of features frequently led to the style being described as 'ship-like' at the time, though in light of how much ships have changed over the past hundred years, this is perhaps less relevant today. Excellent examples include the Northern Hotel, Kittybrewster (1937); **Rosemount Square, Aberdeen** (1938); and the pavilion built in Glasgow, to Spence's design, for the Empire Exhibition of 1938. Like many other Scottish Art Deco buildings, Rosemount Square features streamlined but characteristically stiff-postured animal sculpture: in this case, a horse and rider, though examples

Rosemount Square, Aberdeen

of most of the better-known animals and mythological figures could probably also be found. The overall effect can be quite magnificent, as with the lion of the Aberdeen City War Memorial (1925), but most look like rather unfunny cartoons or the radiator ornaments of gigantic cars. Many Art Deco structures were made of brick or stone, but others made significant use of hitherto unusual exterior materials such as polished marble and concrete. In spite of or because of this, a favourite exterior feature was the **false keystone**. A grandly adorned but small and windowless Art Deco building is fairly likely to have been built as a cinema; these were perhaps ten times more numerous in the interwar years than they are today. There is further discussion of the Art Deco style in section 3–2 below.

False keystone

In contrast to Art Deco, which was associated chiefly with 'fun' in the form of swimming pools, holiday hotels, cinemas, bars and so forth, 'Brutalism' is most associated with governmental build-

An unusual
mixture of Art
Deco elements
(including several
fake keystones)
and Palladian ones
in Edinburgh's
High Court

ings. In particular, it was used for social housing or as army
barracks in the 1960s and '70s – though airports, business
offices, malls and universities all partook of it too. If you
like, it is the architectural expression of the semi-socialist,
semi-puritanical 'nanny state' that was the target of both
Prime Minister Margaret Thatcher and novelist Anthony
Burgess, albeit perhaps from opposite political directions.
It is characterised especially by dense ranks of narrow or
otherwise small-looking windows (of various shapes), and

often by an extreme overall height achieved in prior eras only by cathedrals. In contrast to the backward-looking 'retro' aspirations of the Victorians, '60s Brutalism looked to an imagined, *Jetsons*-like future. Also in great contrast to the buildings of 1840–1920, it was generally poorly built, and saw a return to the lower ceilings and smaller doorways of the pre-1750 era. Its new materials, largely concrete and steel, were produced cheaply and poorly integrated with each other. Many examples are rust-streaked and crumbling rapidly; and a visitor from the very future they were supposed to represent (or create) could be forgiven for thinking they are our oldest, shabbiest and most unenlightened buildings of all.

Brutalism, in its turn, has provoked a reaction, the most obvious aspect of which is that pre-1920 buildings are in far greater demand than later ones, and rise faster and

Too many cooks?

The typical Scottish 'new build' of the 1980s and since is an uneasy mixture of very disparate historical elements: the flattish, Neo-Roman roofline of the early 1800s, the broad eaves of 1880–1910, and the horizontal windows of 1920–40, with an approximation of pre-1750 harling covering all. So while each element can be justified as 'traditional', the net effect is not satisfying to traditionalists or, it seems, to anyone else. Since this style has no name, I will give it one: 'US Air Force Base Postmodernism.'

Keynotes of the brutalist style include massive overall size and large numbers of very narrow windows

higher in price as a result. Since the 1970s and especially since 1990, this in turn has led to intelligent efforts by many architects – but as yet, far too few mass-market home-builders – to reassess what people really *like* about old buildings. Many now strive to create new structures that reflect and inspire these same positive feelings, while at the same time incorporating the ecological and communitarian values that are the main socio-economic and political common ground of Scotland's propertied classes.[32] We are likely to see increasing numbers not just of houses, but of whole communities like Knockroon in East Ayrshire, built to reflect this eco-historical consensus.

3
Cross-Period Issues

Dated stones, arms, initials, masons' marks, insurance marks and site names

Many old Scottish buildings, as well as some very recent ones, carry conspicuous statements of their age in the form of inscribed dates. These are often but not always located above the front door, with a significant minority – particularly from before 1840 – appearing on skewputts (see p. 62). While such stones would seem an obvious guide to a building's age, the dates these stones show are often wildly inaccurate – in either direction. On the one hand, dated stones (with or without coats of arms or owners' initials) were more difficult to carve than ordinary building stones and, because this extra labour was respected by subsequent generations, they were almost never discarded. The datestone of the bridge at the northern end of Aberdeenshire's Glen Tanar estate is from 1779, but it is the only thing of such an age in the bridge, which was actually built in 1894; and scores of similar examples of the re-use of old datestones have been identified. On the other hand, a date was often first applied to a building when it was remodelled or changed owners. For instance, Nether Ardgrain House (pictured p. 44), which was actually built in 1664 for landowner John Moir, carries the date '1731' above the front door, along with the initials of John Bean, the tenant farmer who renovated the house in the latter year. Again, numerous other examples of this practice have been found. At a rough guess, perhaps a third of eighteenth-century dates on Scottish buildings are 'off' by a generation or more, in one direction or the other. Seventeenth- and nine-teenth-century dates tend to be more accurate, but great caution is still necessary; and during the French Revolu-tionary and Napoleonic Wars (1793–1815), for reasons not immediately clear, the use of dates on Scottish buildings virtually came to a halt. Perhaps most importantly, no more than one house in ten seems to have carried a date in the first place, so exhaustive searches for such carvings are unlikely to repay the effort.

Far from dating back to the Romans, who made few inroads in Scotland, building dates in roman numerals here tend to be either from the later sixteenth century, or from 1820 to the present. This is just a rule of thumb, however, and learning to read roman numerals is advisable. Short of learning the entire system, it is worth remembering that dates beginning MCM are twentieth century, MDCCC are nineteenth century, MDCC are eighteenth century, MDC are seventeenth century, and MD (not followed by any Cs) are sixteenth century. The presence of an L, regardless of its position, further implies a date toward the middle of the century in question: specifically, from '40 to '89. Very occasionally, a seventeenth-century roman-numeral date will begin CIƆIƆC, the first three characters being a rough approximation of an 'M' and the fourth and fifth, a 'D'. Where seen, this may be a result of influence from the Netherlands, where this practice was more common.

In the years 1880–1910, it became very popular to install square date-stones on the first-floor level of blocks of flats and offices. Most of these stones simply have a numeral in each corner, which should be read in 'Z' forma-tion rather than clockwise or vertically, i.e.

18
98

is '1898', not '1889' or '1988'. Peculiar variations exist, however, and I have seen '1908' rendered as '098' with a vertical line, representing the '1', struck through the '9'. Fortunately, Scotland does not appear to have followed the South London example of diamond-shaped date-stones that are meant to be read vertically first and horizontally second, e.g.

1

9   6

8

for '1896' and not, as most people would now suppose, '1968', '1986', or even '1689'. Scottish examples of this dubious practice may, however, emerge.

As with monograms on silverware from the same era, stones from 1840–1920 bearing owners' initials will gener-ally put the surname (or the name of the senior partner) in the middle, not at the end as in ordinary writing. Thus the initials of David Edward Sutherland or David and Eliza Sutherland may be 'DSE', not 'DES'; while the firm of Martin, Gordon & Gordon might well be 'GMG'. In such cases, the middle letter is usually slightly taller, which should help remind you of this. Especially prior to 1840, the use of the curving letters 'U' and 'J' in building inscriptions was fairly rare, the straighter letters 'V' and 'I' being substi-tuted.

If you have the good fortune to encounter a fifteenth-century date on a Scottish building, you should bear in mind that **the arabic numeral '4' of that era** was, as compared to the modern '4', tilted 45 degrees to the right: making it look 'like a camp stool', as my friend Jane Geddes

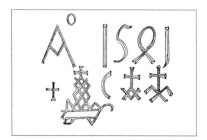

Carving of 'A[nn]o 1541' with a 'half-eight' to represent the 4

once put it. This more clearly reflects the 4's origin as half an 8 (apparently, the top half). It should also be borne in mind that the Arabic '6' used in the seventeenth century often had a very small tail, so small in fact that it can easily be mistaken for a 'o', especially if the carving in question contains no actual 'o' with which to compare it.

A substantial minority of dated stones of the seventeenth and eighteenth centuries, particularly on humbler dwellings, omit the century altogether and give only a year such as '12' or '38', leaving us as usual to diagnose the age of the building from other clues. And just as the dates on lairds' houses may reflect a date of remodelling, or even the date of a previous building that this one replaced, the short-form dates on tradesmen's cottages and farmhouses may represent the marriage date of an occupying couple and not the year of construction. Where this is the case, you will probably also see **two sets of initials, with the groom's on the left and the bride's on the right**. The surname initials are unlikely to match, since many or most Lowland Scots women of the era in question did not take their husbands' surnames. The use of 'marriage lintels' giving initials and the full year seems to have been most popular in the 1660-1750 period, though I have seen quite a few examples dating from long before and long after this: some as early as the first quarter of the sixteenth century.

A carved stone coat of arms on a building tends to indi-

1692 marriage lintel

cate past or present ownership by a person of noble rank, since the use of borrowed or invented arms in Scotland was, and remains, a crime. However, this rule did not apply to the royal arms, the use of which on a non-royal house might indicate nothing more than the owner's patriotism. Therefore, it is worth noting the details of the twelve coats of arms used by Scotland's royal families from the invention of heraldry in the late twelfth century up to the present – even if only to rule them out of consideration when trying to determine the identity of a building's past owner. In some cases, of course, a particular national coat was used for such a short period that it is nearly as useful as a date-stone; and in any case, many heraldic plaques on Scottish buildings also carry dates.

If your interest is in a particular town or village, it is worth learning the arms of its historical leading families. In small villages, these are often prominently displayed on hotels from the late eighteenth and nineteenth centuries called the 'So-and-So Arms', with 'So-and-So' almost inevitably being the surname of the local laird. However, the wrong arms sometimes appear in these situations: the Burnett Arms Hotel in Banchory St Ternan, for instance, actually displays the royal arms of King William IV and his wife, Princess Adelaide of Saxe-Meiningen. Towns and cities above a certain size also mostly have arms of their own, and these tend to be displayed (with varying degrees of prominence) on signage and other municipal property such as iron lamp-posts. Usually, town arms are topped with a crown of bricks – known technically as a **mural coronet** – whereby they can be rapidly distinguished from the arms of both individuals and churches.

Bishops and archbishops of the Episcopal and Catholic churches are granted arms in addition to the unvarying arms of their diocese or archdiocese. These ecclesiastical arms – personal or otherwise – are distinguishable from municipal and non-ecclesiastical personal arms by the presence of a **mitre** or in some cases a **galero** (clerical hat with broad brim and tassels). The number of tassels on the galero indicates the churchman's precise rank, with more tassels indicating a higher position. A non-churchman's personal arms will be topped by one of the many types of non-mural coronet or a stylised knight's helmet or in many cases nothing at all. Unmarried women with the right to bear arms do so on a diamond shape known as a **lozenge** rather than on the shield shape associated with all other heraldry (including that of married women).

Colour is fundamental to heraldry. Without it, it is impossible to distinguish between the shields of Stewart,

Left.
Coat of arms with galero

Right.
Heraldic lozenge, used in place of a shield by unmarried women

Below.
L to r: naval coronet, mural coronet and mitre

DA ROBUR FER AUXILIUM

Lindsay and Boyd (to name just one of many examples). Therefore, stone arms on buildings would originally have been painted. This is rarely kept up, and in the few places where painting does still occur (as in the old quad of King's College, Aberdeen), the correct colours are not always used. Even in monotone, however, the combination of a particular shield with a particular crest – i.e. the part of the design located above the top of the shield[33] – may lead to a correct family identification. The best book on the subject remains Sir Thomas Innes of Learney's *Scots Heraldry* (Edinburgh and London, 2nd edn., 1956), though readers with frequent or difficult questions of this sort are advised to join the Heraldry Society of Scotland, who will have the most up-to-date information.

Up to the mid eighteenth century, Scottish heraldic stone plaques tended to be placed in a **convex stone 'frame'**, typically two to four feet square and standing proud of the wall surface by several inches. In a rural residential building whose other features confirm it as pre-1750, the presence of such a frame is perhaps enough to suggest that the house

Crathes Castle detail showing frames

was built for a noble family as their own residence – even if the arms themselves have been damaged beyond recognition, or removed. Late eighteenth- and nineteenth-century buildings were more likely to display (often much larger) arms without such frames – or, if built after 1840 in a retro-Scottish Renaissance style, to display the frames only, without any arms inside. None of this should be confused with the blank stone shields that are often seen as decoration on later nineteenth-century blocks of flats. These are merely whimsical and do not reflect anything in particular about the owners or builders, though they seem to have been more popular in the south-east of Scotland than elsewhere.

All Scottish masons were ordered to use masons' marks beginning in 1598, though the practice had existed since the Middle Ages. As such, these marks are far too numerous and idiosyncratic to detail in a book of this size; **ten different ones** have been catalogued at Melgund Castle alone. However, it should at least be said that they served two general functions. The first, in a largely pre-literate era,

Scottish masons' marks exhibit a rich variety of shapes, and may be carved or stamped

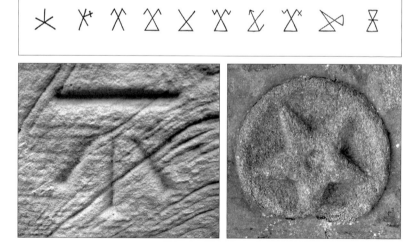

was effectively as a signature. Marks identified who did what in the complex and collaborative building process, for what might now be termed 'Human Resources' reasons: ensuring that the right person was paid for the job, as well as that the job done was of an acceptable standard. The second function was as instructions, of a relatively familiar 'This end up' or 'Handle with care' variety. They can be found either **carved into stone** or **stamped or drawn in wet mortar**, though there is no known relationship between the marks' two distinct purposes and these two distinct methods of creating them. Most are quite small, and would fit easily in a square five inches on a side. If confronted with a pressing need to identify a particular mark, you are advised to submit a picture of it to the Masons' Marks Project of the Scottish Castles Association.

Fire insurance companies and fire brigades both originated in Britain in the late seventeenth century, with the equipment owned and operated by the insurers. Beginning in 1710, a building that was covered by a fire policy might be given a prominent 'insurance plaque' – like this **Sun Fire plaque in Old Aberdeen** – to indicate which insurance company's firemen were responsible for protecting it. These markers are still seen in various parts of the country, including towns of moderate size such as Peebles and Prestonpans.

Sun Fire insurance mark, Old Aberdeen

Made of iron, lead or tin, they tend to consist of a company logo above a five- or six-digit policy number, often mounted above the front door. Edinburgh's fire engines were brought into public ownership in the mid 1820s, and most other Scottish fire services followed suit by the mid 1880s, after which no new insurance

77

plaques should have been put up. However, these items' charm and strong Georgian flavour have led to a small number of convincing replicas being created. It should also be remembered that, while any particular building's plaque must be from after 1709, this does not mean that the building was new at that time (or even that it was uninsured prior to the sign being put up).

Lastly, you should take place-names quite seriously. At least prior to the advent of mass suburbanisation and speculative building aimed at the working classes in the period 1840–1920, the names of streets, roads and individual structures changed slowly and usually reflected their actual function. If something in Scotland is called 'Flourmill Lane' or 'Ropeworks Cottage' or 'Station Brae' or 'Customhouse Street' or 'Blackfriars', it is very likely to be for good reason; and when reading an area's buildings it is better to take these external clues into account than not.

3–2
Marks of quality that transcend period

In addition to those discussed in the previous section on marks, a number of building features cut across two or more of our six broad style epochs. This section deals with details that are more indicative of the *cost and care* lavished on a particular building than of any particular architectural style or era. One of the clearest examples of this is window-surrounds. The least expensive structures in all periods tend to lack these stone 'frames' entirely, and feature window apertures that are no more than holes in an otherwise uniform surface. Houses and inns built at middling cost might feature a prominent stone lintel either immediately above or immediately below each window; while the grandest houses and public buildings of all periods tend to have windows completely enclosed within stone surrounds – or even (at least since 1610) windows with small individual sculptural 'roofs', known technically as pediments. At the most elaborate – e.g. at **Fyvie Castle, Aberdeenshire**, or the courtyard of Argyl's Lodging in Stirling – stone window-surrounds might even include classical columns, sculptured leaves and gargoyles.

Looking beyond window-framing, other signs of quality include **balustrades** (with or without carved stone urns on top); garlands of sculptured foliage; large pediments at roof level; small pediments above doorways; quoins (see pp. 84–85); and – usually only on the ground floor – stone blocks that have been bevelled on all four edges, or only on their top and bottom edges, giving an impression of deep and continuous horizontal grooves (known technically as 'rustication'[34] and illus. on pp. 50 and 66). Between 1870 and

Fyvie Castle, detail of pediments

Seven balusters forming a balustrade

79

Pediment types

the outbreak of the First World War, 'rustication' in particular was a popular feature for theatres, department stores, police stations and banks.

The stylistic package described in the preceding paragraph came to Britain with Inigo Jones in the 1610s. As a whole, it first appeared in Scotland in the work of Sir William Bruce after 1670, though its individual features may be found in pre-Civil War Scottish structures: e.g. the exceptionally **crude quoins** of Craigston Castle (1604–07) or the better, but still far from uniform ones on the east front of Pinkie House (1613). The very beautiful Craigievar Castle (competed 1626), like Craigston, has a balustrade that may or may not be as old as the house itself. The balustrade of Auchans in South Ayrshire dates from between 1644 and 1667, also before Bruce's time; and we have already noted the similarity between the work of Jones and Scottish master mason William Aitoun, who died in 1643.

These relatively superficial signs of high quality, if found in an otherwise humble, relatively small building, may indicate its prior use as a gate lodge, a masonic lodge, a noncon-

Craigston Castle

formist chapel or a master builder's own home. **Master mason Tobias Bauchope's own house in the town of Alloa, 1695,** is a plain ordinary village house in point of size and shape, but is adorned with quoins, fancy 'lugged' window-surrounds, and, above the front door, the sculptural plaque and elaborate wall-sundial more generally associated with the rural mansions of the nobility.

Chimney-stacks with sculptured ridges to their tops, and after 1840, chimney-pots cast in unusual shapes (such as octagons), are also indications that a particular building has been built with an above-average level of care. For a more in-depth discussion of chimney features, see section 4–1, below.

The post-1750 invention of terraces – connected rows of houses designed by a single individual or firm and built all at once – may have led to an increased use of façades, i.e. building fronts that are of finer materials and/or work-manship than the sides. Very often, where an exuberantly grand and smooth-surfaced mid terrace house has been pulled down, it is possible to see that the sides of its identical

neighbours have been built of some completely different and inferior material: roughly squared, splashily mortared puddingstone, say, or brick. The churches built after 1843 by splinter groups from the Church of Scotland are also notorious for this, even though (unlike with terraces) their sides were never meant to be concealed from public view. All that being said, it was of course perfectly possible – at any date – to build an entire building of crude boulder-like elements; so having even one side of finely dressed stone should perhaps be regarded as a point in favour.

Scotland's society and economy have not yet fully recovered from the disaster of the First World War. There are villages on Speyside that have more fallen soldiers' names

End of an early-19th-century terrace, showing a smooth façade joining a crudely constructed side wall

on their 1914–18 war memorials than they have current inhabitants. The '20s did not 'roar' and the '50s did not 'boom'. As also happened with the impoverished post-Reformation Scottish Church, a virtue was made of necessity, and since 1919 Scottish building has adopted a 'stripped down' aesthetic. At times, I personally find the Art Deco style of the 1920s–40s highly appealing – even unto the use of poured concrete as a replacement for carved stone (see section 2–6). Nevertheless, I find it hard to escape the idea that Deco would not have been adopted if the skilled craftspeople – and the funds – needed for a more ornate, labour-intensive architecture had survived our War to End Wars.

Marks of quality

This building, situated in Chatelherault Country Park in South Lanarkshire, typifies the strong urge for symmetry as well as the new 'standardised' signs of grandeur that arose in the period 1660–1750. It lacks a balustrade, but bears all the other superficial marks of an exceptionally fine and costly building, as well as the more fundamental quality of sheer size: though boasting only two storeys, it is as tall as a typical four-storey building of 1700 or three-storey building of 1800. For this reason alone, we can assume it was associated with the 'highest in the land', socially speaking. But how old is it, exactly? The 'blind' windows (p. 160) on the right-hand side are not necessarily evidence that the building predates the Scottish Window Tax of 1748: they are themselves aesthetically pleasing and could have been put there simply to give some interest to a wall that would otherwise be too plain. However, the wall containing these 'blind' windows is harled (see p. 14), strongly suggesting a date before 1770, at least in a structure of this magnificence.

As for the earliest date? The building has highly distinctive door - and window-surrounds, consisting of alternating long and short blocks called quoins. Doorways and windows that employ quoins in this way – especially if coupled with keystones – are called 'Gibbsian', after Aberdeen-born architect James Gibbs, whose first commissions were in the 1710s. Gibbs did not actually invent this, but Scottish uses from before his lifetime (e.g. at Glasgow University) were clumsy and few. Further, the highly distinctive main treble windows on the front of the upper storey are 'Venetian' or 'Palladian' in style (see p. 132), and we know that the first window of this type in Scotland dates to between 1725 and 1730 (p. 154). Finally and most tellingly, the pediments (pp. 80 and 133) on the fronts and sides of both towers are steeply pointed, at least in comparison to actual Roman ones, making it very unlikely they are from after 1750. The building being very much 'of a piece' in terms of materials and style, with no glaringly obvious enlargements or revisions, we can feel fairly safe about assuming that the design is from between 1730 and 1750. A post-1670 building of this quality was ipso facto designed by a notable architect, insofar as a person not famous before designing such a building would certainly have become famous as a result of designing it. Given the 1730–50 date-range – since Gibbs and most of his other London-based Scottish colleagues did little or no work in Scotland – we can assume that the building was by William Adam or his oldest son, John (the other Adam boys being barely out of their teens by the end of the relevant time-window).

That's all very well; but what is it? Great noblemen's houses from this period and the next, in Scotland as in England, were almost always seven windows wide or more. At just five windows wide (the norm for the lesser nobility, politicians and self-made businesspeople), this structure's palace-worthy stylistic grandeur is therefore out of keeping with its overall size. It is also fairly odd, at this or any date, to see two-storey wings flanking a one-storey core. The snap judgement is that it must be a peripheral part of some larger estate: perhaps a home for a great nobleman's widowed mother (technically known as a dower house). But its curiously un-house-like combination of style, size and shape render this diagnosis weak and rather tentative.

A little research confirms that the building dates from 1734 and was designed by William Adam as a hunting lodge, stable and 'dogg kennel' for the Duke of Hamilton (who usually resided at nearby Hamilton Palace, demolished in 1927).

3–3
Symmetry and the notion of 'Georgian style'

Strictly speaking, 'Georgian' is not a style but a period, and a very long one at that, lasting from the accession of King George I in 1714 to the death of his great-great grandson George IV in 1830. In architecture, it is generally extended by a further ten or more years at the end, in order to cover a transitional period before Victorian 'retro' became full-blown (see 'Style 1840–1920', section 2–5 above). Stylistically, the architecture of the Georgian age encompasses the Baroque, Neo-Classical[35] and Neo-Gothic movements – as well as buildings built simply, in imitation of others in their immediate environs, using traditional methods, styles and materials (including clay and thatch) that had altered little since the Middle Ages. Three of these modes of building began before the start of the Georgian era, and all four continued after it ended. **Milne's Court in Edinburgh** could be said to have a typically Georgian appearance, with its plain surface and neat rows of twelve-paned sash windows, but it was completed in 1688, a generation and two full reigns before Georgian times began. Nor is it unusual for buildings of the mid nineteenth century, particularly farmhouses and shops, to project a 'Georgian' quality that is in one sense merely out of date, but in another, a continuation of the tradition of local 'building by eye': see for example the 1845 fish shop, illus. at the far right of p. 46.

What all four modes shared, in stark contrast to both the crooked tower-houses of the pre-1660 period and the eccentric villas of the Victorians, was a profound belief in exterior symmetry. If there is a tower at the east end, it should be answered by a tower of equal size and shape at the west. Front doors went smack in the middle. If there were two windows to the left of the door, there should be

Milne's Court,
Edinburgh

two windows to the right – and, moreover, these groups of windows should be of the same height, width, distance apart, distance from the ground and so forth.

When looking at the front of a house that you already know to be from our third or fourth stylistic periods, i.e. 1660–1840, the smallest degree of asymmetry is a clue that it may have been built not as a dwelling in the first instance, but as a shop, workshop, barracks, coffeehouse (p. 143), school or other 'place of public resort'. For this purpose, somewhat counterintuitively, buildings with a width of an odd number of windows are considered more symmetrical than those with an even number. This is because in a building with an odd frontage, the door can be centred under an upstairs window (e.g. Ardgrain and Balnacraig, p. 44), whereas with an even frontage, the door must either be squeezed uncomfortably between two windows (e.g. Bauchope's house, p. 82), or placed off-centre relative to the house itself. So unless it has been extended laterally, you should consider very carefully whether a building of

Lateral symmetry of residential buildings, 1660–1840

From 1660 to 1840, but at no time before or after, the keynote of Scottish residential architecture was symmetry. The west front of the Palace of Holyroodhouse is symmetrical because in the 1670s, Sir William Bruce added a mirror-image replica of the original 1505 north-west tower to the south-west corner. Provost Skene's House, one of just two sixteenth-century dwellings now standing in New Aberdeen, was also 'regularised' c. 1670.[36] This is Friendville House, Aberdeen, built in 1773.

1660–1840 with a frontage of four or six windows was ever a house. The precise origins of this unwritten rule are lost; but it was arguably the single most powerful idea in play for nearly 200 years, at least when it came to buildings that were not architected per se but simply built.

To this symmetry of design was added a sense that surfaces should be plain. Gargoyles, coats of arms, dated stones, carved owners' initials, gaily-coloured coatings, sundials and all the other delightful peculiarities of the pre-Civil War age declined steadily in popularity over the course

The Palladian or Venetian window

A fine example of a Palladian, a.k.a. Venetian window adorns the upper floor of Innerpeffray Library in Perthshire, Scotland's oldest public lending library, founded in 1680. Such windows were introduced to Scotland after 1725, however: one of the clues that the present building is in fact from 1762. That being said, Palladian windows were occasionally 'punched through' an older structure.

of the eighteenth century, and by 1800 were virtually unknown. Stone was still carved decoratively, particularly the door- and window-surrounds of the finest buildings; but increasingly it reflected the Greco-Roman taste of pattern-book makers like Colen Campbell, rather than the personal idiosyncrasies of masons and owners. Those who do not like buildings from the Georgian age will cite their plainness amounting almost to severity.

Some of you may advance to the point where you will be able to distinguish, within the category of Georgian

Neo-Classical buildings, between and among those that are Palladian, Adam, Greek Revival and Regency. This is mostly a matter of subtle surface decoration, though some structural features – e.g. the Palladian window – are peculiar to one sort or another. It is often said that the first Palladian window in Scotland was designed into Drum House, Gilmerton by William Adam *c.* 1730, though it should be noted that one of the most charming can be seen at Inner-peffray Library (p. 89), as rebuilt in 1762 for Robert Hay-Drummond, Archbishop of York.

3–4
Distinctive buildings of the Scottish countryside

With a handful of exceptions, farmhouses and ministers' manses from before 1660 have conspicuously failed to survive, while the nobility prior to 1660 tended overwhelmingly to live in fortified towers or castles. Farmhouses of 1660–1840 were generally of two storeys with a width of three windows, which distinguished them both from the wider unfortified rural mansions of the lairds that appeared from the 1660s onwards, and from the shorter and narrower farm labourers' cottages of the same era. The majority of surviving manses date from the Improvement Era of 1750–1840, and were built to one of two distinctive patterns. The commoner **two-storey version with a 'hipped' roof and no side windows on the upper floor** is deeper and therefore roomier than farmhouses of the same age. Few manses were turned into farmhouses, because most remained in the possession of the Church until the mid to late twentieth century, when they became expensive and highly sought-after family homes.[37]

Unlike manses, many lairds' mansions did pass into use as farmhouses, particularly during and after the various

West Manse of
Sanday

Jacobite rebellions of 1689–1746, when rebel property was confiscated and politically reliable farmers were imported to rebellious areas from other parts of Scotland and from England. In contrast to purpose-built farmhouses, unfortified lairds' houses were generally built to one of two patterns: 1) two storeys with a width of five windows (e.g. Balnacraig, 1673, illus. on p. 44, or Friendville, 1773, p. 88); or 2) three storeys with a width of three windows (e.g. **Mains of Drummuir**, *c.* 1650). However, a very impoverished laird such as Ochterlony of Tillyfruskie (1733) might well build his mansion in the exact size and external style of a farmhouse of the same age. Aside from library research and conversations with local people, the identification of a smaller-than-usual laird's mansion may come down to it having a heraldic plaque (or the frame for one: see p. 75) above the front door.

Unlike in England, where many 'squires' do not bear arms, Scottish society before the Abolition of Feudal Tenure Act (in force since November 2004) featured a fairly logical 1:1 relationship between noble status and the ownership of extensive rural property. If a laird's principal house were sold, the title of baron or 'of such-and-such' would pass

Mains of
Drummuir

with it to the new owner, even if they were totally unrelated by blood. Most farmers, on the other hand, leased their farms from some member of the nobility, usually for terms of nineteen or thirty-eight years, until after the First World War. And at least in theory, even owners of Scottish buildings prior to November 2004 had a feudal superior – the heir of the original owner of the land on which the house was built – to whom small sums of money had to be paid annually. In part, our cultural absence of a large class of small owner-occupiers akin to the Anglo-American yeomen or French peasant-proprietors ensured that the majority of Scottish rural buildings in all periods would be shabbily and cheaply built, and unlikely to survive in a habitable condition for more than one generation. Those that have survived are therefore all the more to be treasured.

After 1840, farmhouses and lairds' country houses –

though frequently following the trends and tics of 1840–1920 architecture such as broad eaves, 'kneelers' (p. 60), and bay windows – tended to retain the previous era's distinction between a three-window frontage for a farmer and a five-plus-window frontage for a landed gentleman.

Generally found close to or even attached to farmhouses, **steadings** are one-storey structures to house livestock. They are longer, narrower and less tall than Anglo-American or Dutch barns.[38] Since their first widespread appearance in stone in the middle years of the eighteenth century, steadings' style altered little until they were superseded (though far from completely) by prefabricated metal structures after the Second World War. As befits the 1750–1840 origin of most stone steadings still in existence, an ordinary peaked roof with an angle of around 90 degrees should be expected (see also section 4–4, below). However, the height of the wall-head can be as little as five feet; and viewed from directly above, traditional stone steadings may be built in a straight line, a square, an L shape, C shape, H shape or E shape, with the C probably the most usual. If you can gain access to the interior, a cobblestone floor is a good

Typical steading

indication that the building was used to house animals; though on farms still in use as such, many cobbled floors have been covered or replaced with concrete due to government regulations. Occasionally, the buildings of a failed eighteenth-century industrial operation will have been brought into use as steadings: as happened to the 1767 linen-mill at Burnside of Delgaty (illus. in my book *Lost Banff and Buchan*, p. 43). That being said, the use of former lairds' mansions to house chickens, cows and pigs was also far from rare. In the reverse of this phenomenon, hundreds of steadings originally built for livestock have recently been converted into curiously low, narrow family homes – often fitted with sash windows of an older type than the buildings themselves.

As befits their function, purpose-built steadings typically have multiple large doors but few if any windows, and also lack chimneys. However, some steadings from the late eighteenth century onwards incorporated a room for a static steam engine – its position indicated by a single chimney, sometimes of preposterously large size. Church-like small belfries were also sometimes attached to steading buildings to signal the start and end of the work day to labourers in distant cottages and fields.

A single-storey circular building within a steading complex may indicate the presence (or former presence) of a horse-powered engine from the period 1750–1920. The horses, or occasionally oxen, would walk in a circle to turn a vertical shaft, which in turn powered other types of equipment. Much taller circular structures – if they are not chimneys – may be windmill-bases. Because the construction of windmills was not economically viable for typical farms of under 500 acres (the average farm size in Scotland even today is slightly under 250 acres), windmill-bases are usually associated with larger landed estates. However, a handful can be seen in towns, for instance

Fraserburgh, where they were built by industrial-scale grain-milling or saw-milling operations of the later eighteenth century. A chimney with a 'hat' of the type made famous by the distilling industry, if found on a farm, probably indicates the site of a corn-drying kiln; understandably, the illicit stills famously operated by Scotland's small farmers up to the 1880s have left almost no architectural traces.

Classic distillery roof shape

Tiny steps up to a door too small for any human being may indicate the part of a steading (or other rural building) that was used as a henhouse. Doves, introduced to Lowland Scotland in the eleventh century by the Norman nobility, were also raised in purpose-built houses, known here as doocots. The birds were chiefly a source of meat, though their droppings were also collected and used as cloth dye, leather dye and fertiliser. Doocots were a noble monopoly, 'simple to establish, easy to operate, productive in the first year, protected by law and, best of all, the pigeons fed ... at the expense of the serfs [i.e. on the grain growing in the serfs' fields]'.[39] A second offence of stealing from a Scottish nobleman's doocot was punishable by amputation of the right hand. The architecture of doocots varies enormously, but most are round or square in plan, and about the height of a two-storey human dwelling. Unlike English dovecots, Scottish doocots are not usually attached to any other structure. All have one or more doors for the use of their human keepers, and most have at least a few visible small square holes for the birds to enter and exit. However, windows of a more usual type are rare. The **earliest doocots** (pre-1600) usually resemble giant beehives, with Rendall Doocot on Orkney Mainland (1648) being a very late example of this type. **Later ones** are more like tiny tower-houses.

Above left.
Early beehive
doocot

Above right.
A late, square
doocot

Right.
Ice house

Doocots fell out of use suddenly and permanently during the 1750–1840 period, when 'enlightened' landlords came to see them as embarrassing relics of feudal oppression.

A very small, isolated, one-storey structure with a single doorway and no windows, especially if semi-subterranean, may be an **ice house**. Lined with straw and packed with ice gathered from natural sources, these were used on nobles' estates to refrigerate food during the summer. All surviving ones seem to date from after 1650, though they continued to be built and used for more than a century after the first successful experiments in artificial refrigeration (William Cullen of Glasgow University having made the first ice by artificial means in 1756).

3–5
Who owned old Scottish buildings?

As previously mentioned, noble status and landownership in Scotland went hand in glove for centuries. It is therefore a bit pointless to argue that the nobles had a monopoly of land, for in the sixteenth through eighteenth centuries, any Scot who earned a large enough sum of cash through trade, high seas adventure, or long governmental or military service would generally buy an estate as soon as possible, and be counted as noble (legally if not socially) from that day forward.[40] An estate needed workers and domestic servants, all of whom typically lived on-site, and – down to the middle of the eighteenth century – many estates had an additional element of 'muscle', i.e. private military forces. In the Highlands, this military aspect was highly formalised, with a middle class known as *tacksmen* having the largest farms and serving as officers in the clan regiments; but with the abolition of private armies after 1746, this class disproportionately emigrated to British North America, and they have left few architectural traces here. In the Lowlands up to the same date, the houses of the poor were generally built by the occupiers themselves, at their own (often meagre) expense, on the land of a noble who might or might not also be their employer. These tenants knew that they might be asked to leave at any time, or at any rate at the end of any nineteen-year lease period. Some noble landlords, for instance the Farquharsons of Invercauld, were as famous for never throwing a tenant out as the Duke of Sutherland was for throwing them out by the boat-load – part of a national phenomenon remembered with a shudder as the Clearances. The labour-saving 'Age of Improvement' in agriculture, the end of private armies, the Industrial Revolution, prolonged wars against France and the United States, the Clearances, a near-famine (in 1782–83), and voluntary emigration to the colonies all coincided in a 'perfect storm' in the period 1750–1840, and all contributed significantly to rural depopulation.

Paradoxically, perhaps, this depopulation led to a dramatic improvement in the housing conditions of those rural workers who remained in Scotland: their houses were now for the first time built largely of mortared stone, and often provided as a part of their compensation package (as had been the case with ministers' manses for two centuries). This period and the next, i.e. 1750–1920, saw the phenomenon of whole estates – lairds' houses, workers' cottages, bridges, monuments, gate lodges and even stables – conceived by a particular mind and built in a particular style. Penicuik (1699–1755) is a fine, very early example of this, and Glen Tanar (1869–85) an excellent late one. Glen Tanar in particular was conceived with labourers' well-being in mind, much along the lines of England's 'model' planned communities for the workers of certain industrial firms, such as Bournville (1893–1900), built in Birmingham for Cadbury. However, on many estates and

most smaller farms, large same-sex groups of unmarried field-hands continued to be housed in primitive barracks called 'bothies'. They are typically larger and squarer in plan than the classic single-storey, two-roomed **'but and ben' cottages** that were built (albeit usually on leased land) by and for rural family units. Farmworkers' bothies, however, should not be confused with mountaineers' and fishermen's bothies, which are used only for short-term temporary shelter, and which are often rebuilt from the ruins of but-and-ben cottages. The word itself is merely a corruption of *bothag*, Gaelic for 'hut', 'booth' or 'shack'.[41]

Thatched but-and-ben cottage with one stone and one wooden chimney

In urban areas, another new phenomenon that originated in the 1750–1840 period was the speculative building of houses, streets and whole neighbourhoods, in hopes that residents for them could soon be found. Beautiful, to be sure, but also faintly anonymous, the New Town of Edinburgh (1767–*c* 1840) was merely the largest of many such projects of the age, including the 1805–42 rebuilding of New Aberdeen in a similar style (e.g. **Golden Square, 1810–21**). After 1840, speculative building extended further down

Golden Square,
Aberdeen

the social scale: increasingly targeting the prosperous lower middle class and skilled industrial workers, rather than just the well-to-do, as before. Mortgages were still unusual, however: in the early nineteenth century, they still fulfilled their original medieval function of providing 'bail-out' money to the landed elite, taking land they had inherited as security for a cash loan for some specific, often non-land-related purpose. The idea that landless people below the gentry level could use the same sort of legal instrument to acquire property 'on tick' was essentially a new phenomenon of 1840–1920; and to a great extent, the types of houses that were built in the period – especially, small terraced houses[42] – reflect this.

Unless they had inherited land and/or large sums of money, many members of the professional upper-middle class of lawyers, doctors, military officers, senior civil servants and so forth continued to rent their houses up until the First World War. Since the coming of the railways in the 1840s, moreover, they had acquired the habit of renting a *different* house in the summer, further from their place of business, and commuting to work by train while their families relaxed in the cleaner air of the countryside. A surprising proportion of the stately late nineteenth-century villas of Aboyne, Aberdeenshire (to name just one example) were built specifically as summer lets for prosperous city dwellers. This answers the architectural riddle of how a remote village of fewer than a thousand people, needing – in the general course of things – no more than one doctor, one dentist, two clergymen and three schoolteachers, could apparently support a professional class of two hundred persons or more. Such purpose-built rentals generally have a second, much smaller and less well constructed house in the back garden, into which the actual owners retreated when the Summer People came.

Today, with acquisition of land via mortgages having become normal for all classes, we can perceive a curious phenomenon that might be called 'owner inflation'. A teacher would now consider him- or herself fortunate to live in a house built for a gardener, weaver or groom a century or two ago. The sort of house that was built for a teacher back then can now only be afforded by a doctor or dentist, while the houses built for doctors can only be afforded by bankers and the houses built for bankers only by rock musicians or corporations. And I would be surprised if one in thirty members of the aristocracy – including those still in possession of their estates – could nowadays afford to buy an estate on the open market.

3–6
Reading a house built in a number of periods:
the case of Lauriston Castle

Surviving buildings from before 1840 have almost always
been subject to major modifications. Sometimes these additions, subtractions and 'facelifts' hide the original house
completely, but often the older and newer elements sit side
by side. Look carefully at this picture of **the south front of
Lauriston Castle**, located in Cramond Road, Edinburgh.
To an extent, it appears to be a unified design. But the
porch at the centre is constructed of a smooth, uniformly
reddish stone, suggesting a later date than the rough-hewn
and multi-coloured boulders of the taller structure on the
left. Looking directly upward from the porch itself, we see
that the masonry in the triangular area between the crowsteps (see section 4–2) has been painstakingly made to look
artisanal and random, but in fact its blocks are far more
regular and square than those of the taller structure beside
it. The shallow point of the arched doorway leading into
the porch is stylistically English Tudor, which in Scotland
suggests a date after 1750. The porch's ground-floor pair
and first-floor trio of identical windows, separated only
by thin vertical stone bars, suggest a date after 1840 (sections
4–14 and 4–15); so does the notable evenness of the crowsteps. The sculptural plaque immediately above the 'Tudor'
archway looks insufficiently weather-beaten to be from
before the nineteenth century. There being essentially
nothing left of the porch area to examine, we can conclude
it is from after 1840.

Moving on towards the left, the first thing that should
strike us (beyond the large, irregular and multi-coloured
blocks of masonry previously mentioned) is the incredible
variety of window sizes, shapes, positions and fittings. Note
also how steeply pointed the roof is, as compared to the

roof behind the porch – which itself is fairly steep by post-1750 standards. We can see two frames for coats of arms or other sculpture, both of pre-1750 type. There is an arch, added merely for strength, between the two principal windows of the first floor, some fifteen feet above the ground; and in keeping with buildings from 1750 and earlier the first floor is at least five, perhaps eight feet closer to the ground than the first floor of its nineteenth-century immediate neighbour. High up on the ground floor, between the two sculpture-frames, there is an ugly blocked window that could not possibly have been added for the sake of symmetry or aesthetics, suggesting that this part of the building had already come into existence before the window-tax of 1748. The abrupt interruption of the crow-steps by a turret, top floor left, is unlikely to have appealed to Victorian fans of retro-Baronialism, suggesting that the turret, and the crowsteps themselves, are both pre-1840 – and therefore probably pre-1750, since crowsteps were hardly used at all between 1750 and 1840. The turrets' tiny, lattice-paned windows no bigger than a man's face, and the larger (but still not large) dormer windows that rise from the wall-head into elaborately sculptured points are, like the roofline itself, correct for the period 1540–1660. Such dormers were scarcely seen again before the 1840s, when W.H. Playfair (1790–1857) appears to have re-introduced them, though they remained popular for higher-quality buildings thereafter, particularly in the hands of architect Sir Robert Lorimer (*fl.* 1885–1916). In style, therefore, and probably also in fact, the left-hand structure is from the 1540–1660 period. The only factors suggesting otherwise include the three first-floor windows – whose sizes and shapes are more appropriate to *c.* 1800–40 – and the chimneys, which though completely correct for a grand Scottish building from the first half of the seventeenth century (see section 4–1), are oddly new-looking. A little

Lauriston Castle, Edinburgh

digging in the database of the Royal Commission on the Ancient and Historical Monuments of Scotland (RCAHMS)[43] confirms this rough-and-ready diagnosis: Lauriston is a tower-house from about 1600, with a porch by Mr Playfair added in 1845, and major recent restoration work to the original chimneys.

But RCAHMS is mute with regard to the third visible part of the house, i.e. to the right of Playfair's porch. More so than the porch area, this right wing seems to tie together stylistically with the tall sixteenth-century block at the far left. It is more similar in colour and texture, with none of the porch's smooth, red stone. It has a similar turret, and similar dormer windows with sculptured stone triangles pointing to the sky. But all of this is superficial. The shallow roof-peak, of about 90 degrees, and wide, plain chimney-stack both suggest the period 1750–1840. The three windows with the points are positively enormous – as tall as a tall man – suggesting a date after 1800, when steam power was first applied to glass manufacture (see p. 148). However, the 'retro' use of oversized dormers of this style started even later: probably with Playfair's design for New College, Edinburgh, in 1846. The turret is suspiciously smooth, and suspiciously near to the ground. Finally, the ground floor's trio of identical windows, separated only by thin vertical stone bars, would have come into vogue certainly after 1840 and probably after 1890. Thus, on the roofline and chimney-stack evidence, we see a plain, farm-house-like building of about 1800, which on the window evidence may have been 'facelifted', much later in the nine-teenth century, so as to more closely resemble the original tower house at the far left. However, the porch and the 'facelift' of the right wing – though of approximately the same age – are different enough from each other that they were almost certainly executed by different architects. We know from RCAHMS that Playfair's greatest rival, William

Burn (1789–1870), worked on the house in 1827; but nothing visible in this picture resembles Burn's work of that decade, unless it is the balustraded west front that we can see just peeking around the left-hand corner of the old tower house. So, the authorship of the 'facelift' remains a mystery; but then, when reading a Scottish building, something always does.

4
From the Top Down: Reading the Elements of a Scottish Building

4–1
Above the roof 1: chimney-stacks and pots

Often, due to trees, hedges, boundary walls and other miscellaneous obstacles, you will not be able to see much of a particular structure. Inevitably, when this happens, the part you are able to see is the upper part. It therefore makes sense to train yourself to examine every building from the top down. Fortunately, Scottish roofs are packed with information.

Prior to 1660, very large houses with many fireplaces might have either a great many relatively small chimneys (e.g. at Innes House, illus. on pp. 37 and 107); or a much smaller number of wide, dominant chimney-stacks (as at **Glenbuchat Castle, 1590**). This does not seem to have had any strong regional pattern, though the most expensive Scottish noblemen's houses from *c.* 1600–60, and university buildings of the same date, tended to have gaggles of more decorative single-flue chimneys in preference to plain multi-flue stacks of monstrous size. The latter may have already been seen as unfashionably medieval. The best houses and public buildings from the first half of the seventeenth century tend to have groups of tall, narrow, square chimneys angled at 45 degrees to the footprint of the house.

Glenbuchat
Castle

Alternatively, aristocratic chimney-clusters could be carved into a variety of fantastical shapes, such as the **rope-like spirals** of Winton House, East Lothian (1620–27), or the **concave-sided octagons** of Heriot's Hospital (1628–42). Labourers' cottages at the same date would have a single chimney built into a gable-end, or a wooden one suspended from the centre of the roof. Purpose-built retail

Winton House,
East Lothian

A jaunty angle

Square chimneys, angled 45 degrees to the foot-print of the house, were characteristic of finer Scottish buildings from the early to mid seventeenth century. This is Innes House, Morayshire; but see also our picture of Lauriston on pp. 104–5.

Left.
Heriot's Hospital,
Edinburgh

Right.
Blucher Hall,
Levenhall

shops, pubs and primary schools were as yet unknown, all such activity at the time still being run out of municipal buildings or private dwellings, or in the open air.

Surviving buildings of the period 1660–1750 typically have square or very slightly rectangular chimney-stacks, containing one or two flues; and unlike their pre-1660 cousins, these are not placed at a 45-degree angle to the building's foundation. In further contrast to their angled predecessors, they tended to emerge only from gables, not the wall-head. In the very best houses, chimney-stacks now terminated not in a plain 'lip', as was usual before, but in a beefy trapezoidal shape known as 'coving': see p. 109. Many of the better houses of this period also tended to have their chimney-stacks outlined in thin lines of smooth stone that were not covered with harling. In the following period up to 1840, though harling fell out of favour with the aristocracy and gentry, this type of decorative stone margin continued to be a mark of quality on 'middle class' chimneys that were still harled, as on the **Blucher Hall in Levenhall** (1814).

Unwanted chimneys have usually been blocked up rather than removed. Therefore, an undersupply or absence of chimneys is generally your first and best clue that a building was from the outset non-residential: a workshop, storehouse, steading, chapel, etc. However, as discussed with regard to p. 32, a single grossly oversized chimney may also indicate a forge, bakery or other type of fire-dependent workshop.

Coving

Taller-than-average 'coved' chimney-tops adorn this otherwise fairly typical urban residence of a prosperous merchant or lesser noble from the period 1660–1750. Plainer, but still nearly square two-flue stacks can be seen on a house of c. 1690 on p. 26, right, immediately behind the mercat cross of Airth. The visible chimney-pots of the Airth house are unusual for such an early date, and may have been added later.

Gill's Lodging, Fraserburgh

Over the course of the wider period 1660–1840, chimney-stacks tended to become rectangular rather than square – largely because they contained more flues apiece. In buildings of average size, such as merchants' townhouses, coffeehouses and small inns, two or fewer flues per stack was the norm at the beginning of the period, and four or more was the norm at the end. As with increased window size (see section 4–10 below), this was in part due to the advent of cheap coal. Over the course of the period 1750 to 1840, coincident with the Industrial Revolution, British production of coal expanded threefold, and its retail price fell by 30 per cent in real terms. Suddenly, after centuries of struggling to find enough peat or wood to sustain an average of just 1.2 to 1.5 hearths per home,[44] a dramatic expansion in the number of fireplaces per Scottish house had become economically plausible. Domestic servants were also in higher demand at the end of the period than at the beginning, and thus were more able to obtain basic creature comforts in their own quarters. Even the humble cottages of the labouring poor tended to acquire a single-flue chimney-stack at each end during this period, as the classic 'but and ben' cottage evolved from earlier, one-chimneyed oval- or semi-oval designs. These will be discussed further in section 4–19, 'Walls 2: walls that lean or curve', below.

Another change between 1660 and 1840, and particularly after 1750, was the advent of terracotta chimney-pots that could be seen from ground level. Assuming that they have not merely lost their pots due to some accident, chimneys that appear to be 'potless' are often from the first half of the eighteenth century or earlier. By the 1840s, the proliferation of purpose-built pubs, banks, blocks of flats, office-blocks and hotels ensured the return of truly mighty chimney stacks, some containing a dozen flues or more; in **extreme cases**, these are so wide that the building's end gables appear almost square.

A single chimney-stack wide enough to accommodate 13 flues, early 19th century

4–2
Above the roof 2: crowsteps

In Britain and the Commonwealth, crowsteps are widely seen as an authentic Scottish feature, but they are likely to have come here from Denmark or the Low Countries, where they appeared up to two centuries earlier. It may be significant that Falkland in Fife (1501–41), a Renaissance palace 'earlier of its kind than anything in England',[45] has crowsteps that are not 'steps' at all, but **knife-edged like the Dutch and Flemish originals**. Post-1540 Scottish crowsteps, like those of Denmark and southern Sweden, are more likely to be flat-topped. One of the most frequently faked features in Scottish architecture after 1840, crowsteps nevertheless have some diagnostic value.

The key points to remember are as follows: crowsteps were frequently applied before and after, but almost never during, the period 1750–1840; the 'old-growth' or pre-1750 type are likely – like early rooflines more generally – to be steep; and occasionally, early crowsteps at the front

Knife-edged crowsteps at Falkland Palace

of a house will join the chimney at a higher or lower point than those at the back. This was a type of irregularity that the Victorians shunned, copying it rarely, if at all.

Very large buildings of the early seventeenth century, such as Pinkie House and Heriot's Hospital, often have flights of crowsteps that continue upwards from interior walls, bisecting and interrupting a roof that the Victorians would have left smooth. Another very old feature that the retro brigade have tended to shun is the placement of crowsteps on one end of a building but none at the other end. And a single 'flight' of very old crowsteps may also contain steps of varying heights. Lastly, and perhaps most importantly, 'less is more'. Any use of crowsteps on dormer windows is usually late/inauthentic: 'cat-slides' or non-stepped triangles having prevailed almost universally as dormers in the seventeenth century – even on houses that are otherwise liberally covered in crowsteps, such as Argyll's Lodging, Stirling

Argyll's Lodging, Stirling

Pre-1750 crowsteps

Authentic crowsteps of the pre-1750 period often 'fail to join up', meeting the chimney at different heights. However, this is not to suggest that all those which do 'join up' are later: indeed, many quite ancient flights of crowsteps are very precisely made. Conversely, post-1920 masters of 'retro' did occasionally fake this type of irregularity, as Sir Basil Spence did at Broughton Place in the mid 1930s.

(1632–74; illus. opposite) and Hamilton House, Prestonpans (1626).

Notwithstanding the prominence I have given to this topic, please remember that Scottish buildings without any crowsteps were also built in all parts of the country and in all time periods.

4–3
Above the roof 3: battlements and crenellations

Battlements consisting of an alternating series of uprights (known as *merlons*) and notches (*crenels*) are, one would suppose, the signature characteristic of medieval architecture. A privilege of the crown, and strictly guarded, the right to 'crenellate' a property had to be specifically granted: as for instance to John Dundas of that Ilk, with reference to his castle at Inchgarvie, in 1491.

With the end of civil warfare, mass rebellion and widespread banditry, the sense of battlements as a royal prerogative slowly relaxed, and they became purely decorative. **Inveraray Castle in Argyllshire** received them for the first time in 1744 at the hands of Colen Campbell's English protégé, Roger Morris (1695–1749). James Adam then redesigned Douglas Castle in South Lanarkshire in an airy mock-medieval style in 1757.[46]

By the 1770s, this style had become widely fashionable. 'New-build' crenellated structures from the reign of George III include Wedderburn Castle (1770–76), Mellerstain House (1770–78), Taymouth Castle (1801–12), Airth Castle (1807–09), Crawford Priory (1809–12), Hatton Castle in Aberdeenshire (1814), **Dalmeny House** (1814–17), the Calton Hill felons' prison (1815–17), Newbyth House (1817), Tulliallan Castle (1817–20), Duns Castle (1818–22), and Abbotsford (1817–24) – with Abbotsford being

Inveraray Castle

Dalmeny House

the 'missing link' between this style and the later Scottish Baronial Revival. Psychologically, the pseudo-castle craze may have been driven by the global forty-year struggle against American and French republicanism; but in a more immediate sense, it was sparked off by Morris's design[47] for Inveraray. I am not given to crying 'Anglocentrism', but the persistent tendency to call Strawberry Hill House in Twickenham, England the first Neo-Gothic house in Britain is questionable at best, given that it was begun five years after Inveraray, and indeed, after Inveraray's architect had died.

Not all post-1750 mock-castles were newly built, of course. The current, crenellated appearance of Darnaway, inhabited since the thirteenth century, dates only to 1810, and that of fifteenth-century Drummond Castle is the result of remodelling by George Kennedy in the 1840s and '50s; while the crenellations of fifteenth-century Broughty Castle near Dundee were added by the War Department in 1861. Similar examples could be multiplied endlessly, but in the absence of a known royal (as distinct from merely noble) connection, one should assume that a Scottish house's battlements are from 1750 or later until proved otherwise; **Lochryan House in Wigtownshire (1701)** is a particularly remarkable exception proving the rule.

Further to this, battlements in which the *merlons* and *crenels* are almost exactly the same size as one another are usually from after 1750. Those with V-shaped notches in the tops of the *merlons* – i.e. which aspire to be Spanish or Italian – are also probably post-1750. So are *merlons* with double steps, e.g. on the porch and main tower of Blairquhan Castle (as redesigned in 1820 by William Burn).

Lochryan House

Non-'retro' Scottish examples – as at the Great Hall and Forework of Stirling Castle; Holyrood Palace; Falkland Palace; Balgonie Castle (Fife); Rusco Tower (Kirkcudbrightshire); and Pinkie House, Musselburgh – almost always have *merlons* that are much wider than the *crenels* that separate them. But even these examples are from the sixteenth and seventeenth centuries, not the Middle Ages per se. So, paradoxically, the one architectural feature most popularly associated with medieval siege warfare is perhaps our clearest indication that a Scottish building is *not* medieval. It is questionable whether Archibald Elliott (1760–1823), architect of Newbyth, even intended for it to look medieval, as opposed to Middle Eastern or simply imaginative. It is this light, fairy-tale quality that separates the Georgian mock-castles – especially those by William Burn – from the Victorian ones.

Even farmers' concrete water towers are frequently given mock crenellations in Aberdeenshire, while any single-storey building with crenellations is likely to be a nineteenth-century gate lodge. Parish churches with crenellated square towers – commonplace in England – are virtually unknown in Scotland, where this style is generally limited to the wealthier cathedrals and abbeys of the fifteenth century (see section 4–7 below). Monymusk Priory, though dating back to Norman times, had its crenellations added as recently as 1891, as part of a deliberate programme of Anglicisation.

4–4
The normal Scottish roof

As you have probably already noticed, the most commonly seen type of roof on an old Scottish building is a simple peak, made from grey slate, and running between two pointed end-walls known as gables.[48] In the year 1700 in towns, it was usual for gable-ends to point at the street, i.e., for the roof-ridges of the houses (seen from above) to be roughly perpendicular to the street and roughly parallel to one another. By 1800, the fashion for town planning had shifted to the modern arrangement, in which roof-ridges form a more or less continuous line parallel to the street (even where the street itself is curved), and most gable-ends are hidden by one another. The old way, it was said in the 1790s without further explanation, 'offends the eye of the traveller'.[49] In urban settings, therefore, a building with its chimney end pointing into the street rather than at the neighbouring house may well be a survivor from the 1660–1750 period, or perhaps even longer ago. This was never a general rule, however, and you should never decide that a house is from after 1750 simply because its roof-ridge and the street are parallel. Conversely, many fishing

Pre-Enlightenment town plan with gable ends facing the street

villages continued to be built gable-ends-to-street for gener-ations after the 1750s, by which time the linear pattern had become firmly established elsewhere. And by 1900, 'retro' stylists had rediscovered the charm of pointing gable ends toward the street; so this alignment should never be taken, by itself, as proof-positive of great age.

Despite the many drawbacks of thatched roofs, no alter-native to them was foreseen as the seventeenth century drew to close. In most parts of the country, a minority of farmhouses and the majority of farmworkers' cottages were still thatched as late as 1840. The progression of the use of slate on even very humble buildings was very rapid after that date, however, and indeed it had begun as early as 1780 in areas where naturally occurring slate was plentiful, such as Tweeddale and Traquair. Because they were locally sourced whenever possible, regional variations in colour, breadth and thickness of the slates are readily discerned. Nevertheless, slate roofs have no particular diagnostic value since, like sash windows (see section 4–10 below), they have been applied retrospectively to structures of every conceivable age, quality and purpose.

In the case of a roof shaped like a pyramid or truncated pyramid (see section 4–5, 'Non-standard roofs 1', below), small overhanging eaves are virtually inevitable and not especially significant. However, in a traditional single-peaked Scottish roof, overhanging eaves that completely hide the tops of the gable-ends are almost all post-1840 and probably post-1880. The very oldest houses, mean-while, tend to have gable-ends (often in the form of crow-steps: see section 4–2, above) that rise higher than the roof-ridge. Between these two extremes, and between the years 1660 and 1840, roofs and gables tended to fit more or less neatly together, with neither component dominating the other. Put another way: the older the style of a house, the taller its gables are likely to be relative to the roofing material, and the less likely they are to be covered/overhung by it.

Widely overhanging eaves, in any type of roof, are virtually impossible to find in Scottish buildings from before 1800, perhaps because their drainage function was fulfilled by thatch; while the Scottish townhouses built with overhanging eaves and slate or timber-plank roofs in the Jacobean period (1587–1625) have almost all been remodelled beyond recognition or destroyed. As this feature of a building is rather fundamental and difficult to change, a house with broad overhanging eaves (on a roof that is not a 'hipped' or 'piend' of the Queen Anne style: see next section) should be assumed to be post-1840 until proved otherwise.

The angles of the peaks of standard Scottish roofs varied greatly over time, and it is tempting to see a correlation between particular roof angles and particular periods. Pre-1750 roofs have a strong tendency to be very steep, usually with a ridge angle of less than 80 degrees (p. 29, top, and p. 111). From the mid eighteenth century to the mid nineteenth, an angle of almost exactly 90 degrees was the fashionable norm – though some unfashionable, usually commercial buildings such as Edinburgh's lost luckenbooths had roof-angles of 120 degrees or more. Perhaps under the influence of the ever-larger numbers of bookishly neo-Roman buildings built here after 1750, flatter roof angles of up to 140 degrees, loosely reminiscent of ancient Roman pediments, came to be seen even in humble urban dwellings and shops.

That being said, it should be noted that Church architecture often lagged behind domestic architecture by a generation or more. This is most evident in the persistence of steep (less than 80-degree) rooflines after shallower (more than 90-degree) roofs became standard for most other types of buildings,[50] even including steadings built for livestock.

In examining roof angles, you will also quickly begin to notice mismatched masonry where **an old, steep roof has been built up to 90 degrees or more**, to keep up with the fashion while simultaneously adding space to attic areas. Likewise, a great many Scottish buildings, particularly those built in the Georgian era as single-storey shops, were extended upward by a full storey or more in the mid/late nineteenth century to accommodate growing families and/or paying residential tenants (see also section 4–8, 'Walls 1: string courses and corbelling', below). As such, their rooflines may post-date the main structure by a hundred years or more. But by and large, when looking at a group of

House from the 1730s with extensive structural alterations (including roof angle), made to keep pace with the latest trends

non-ecclesiastical buildings that you know to be from before 1840, the steepest roofs are likely to be the oldest. After 1840, as 'retro'-mania took pride of place in Scottish architecture, all bets were off, and roof-angles were no longer particularly useful as a guide to age. Indeed, theorists of Neo-Gothic architecture urged a return to steepness.

A Scottish slate roof of any shape may feature red terracotta roof-ridges, sometimes quite plain but often in a repeating pattern of points, knobs or square fins. This feature marks the building as having been built (or remodelled) after 1840, and probably between 1860 and 1900. Buildings whose entire roof is made of tile, however, will have tile roof-ridges as a matter of course, and may be of any age. Even in the brief period when red terracotta roof-ridges were popular, however, the majority of roof-ridges

Early 20th-century commercial building, with crowstepped and 'Dutch' dormers and a brick end-wall.

remained grey slate or lead, so the absence of terracotta ridges should not be seen as especially significant.

The most fashionable and expensive tower houses of the sixteenth and seventeenth centuries had 'pitched roofs of thick stone slabs',[51] but the majority were slated – at least by the period 1750–1840, during which slate became normal for the majority of Scottish roofs, including those that had previously been thatched.

4–5
Non-standard roofs 1: semi-pyramids, pyramids and curvilinear designs

True pyramid roofs have been used in Scotland since at least the seventeenth century on buildings with a wide range of functions and levels of social pretension. They have appeared on the outer wings of grand country houses like Balcaskie (as remodelled by Sir William Bruce from 1668) and Kinneil House (1675–86), and the picturesque garden

The current
ogee roofs of
Pitmedden's
garden pavilions
replaced earlier,
pyramid roofs

pavilions at Pitmedden (1686), as well as on potting sheds,
static-steam-engine houses, chapels, watch-houses, one-car
garages and other miscellaneous rural outbuildings not
generally thought of as habitable. Pyramid roofs are also
relatively easy to retro-fit to small, square-ish buildings of
any age. As such, they have no particular diagnostic value.

However, an important variant of the pyramid, most
popular in the time of King Charles I (r. 1625–49), is the
'ogee' roof with four equal straight sides in the base, but
delicate curves where the four sides meet. Six-sided and
eight-sided 'ogee' roofs are also sometimes seen here.
Strongly reminiscent of the roofs on the corners of the
White Tower of the Tower of London, 'ogee' roofs have
adorned the west range of St Mary's College, St Andrews
(begun 1563), Winton House (1620–27), Heriot's Hospital
(1628–42) and the Scots Parliament building of the 1630s
(since destroyed by fire), as well as spectacular Victorian-
era 'retro' replications such as Donaldson's College (1851;
pictured p. 57). 'Ogee' roofs have also replaced the original

pyramid roofs at Pitmedden Garden, as part of restoration work undertaken since 1952. Usually made of slate, copper or lead, they have occasionally been executed in solid stone – for instance, on Aberdeen's Castlegate Well and Musselburgh's War Memorial. Given their appearance here after the Protestant Reformation, when Scotland spurned France and became allied to Elizabethan England, it would not be a great leap to ascribe the sudden popularity of 'ogee' roofs to English cultural influence; though as always, Danish influence via Anna (queen consort to James VI from 1589 to 1619) should not be overlooked. Six- and eight-sided ogee roofs, in particular, were highly popular in Denmark from 1575 to 1650.

All-metal, octagonal ogee roof, Edinburgh, c. 1640

Unlike the true pyramid roof, which covers a bewildering range of often quite mundane or menial structures, a truncated pyramid – particularly with a balustraded observation platform on top – has always been associated with grander buildings here. Very shallow truncated pyramids, as at Shawfield (p. 42), are particularly associated with the Late Stuart period (1660–1714), while **very tall and steep ones** are the signature feature of the so-called French Gothic style that was most popular in Scotland from 1860 to 1890.

Seen from a distance and from certain angles, truncated pyramid roofs can be hard to distinguish from rectangular roofs composed of triangles at the sides and trapezoids at front and rear. This so-called 'hipped' or 'piend' shape was first seen in Scotland at the end of the seventeenth century, thanks again to Sir William Bruce. It is perhaps especially associated with the time of our last Stuart queen, Anne (*r.*

1702–14), though it has been used in a minority of relatively grand buildings ever since. The earliest surviving eaves in non-thatch form are part of truncated-pyramid roofs from *c.* 1700, and are hardly very wide by post-1840 standards.

The **'half-hipped' or 'earflap' roof**, known throughout northern Europe and still the dominant rural roof type in the Dutch province of Utrecht, was popular in Scotland only from 1900 to 1930, chiefly for small public buildings such as village hospitals and schools, but sometimes for houses as well. Of far earlier and more enduring popularity was the curvilinear or 'Dutch' gable. To call these various structures 'Dutch' is particularly un-apt, as those seen in Scotland are as likely to be Swedish, Danish, Italian or even Spanish in inspiration. The **shaped gables**

Above.
Tall, steep truncated-pyramid roofs were the signature element of Scotland's 'French Gothic' style of the later 19th century

Right.
An early (c. 1680) example of the 'hipped' or 'piend' roof

of David Bryce's Old Surgical Hospital, Edinburgh (1853), with scrolls on the sides and pediments on top, are clearly intended to evoke sixteenth-century Italy – though in fairness, many gables in the Netherlands attempt to do the same. The **East Kirk of Rathen (1843–44)**, in contrast, is astonishingly Spanish- or even Mexican-looking. With regard to houses, the epicentre of the 'Dutch' gable fashion was in the environs of Edinburgh on medium-sized gentry dwellings of the seventeenth century – for instance **Pilrig (1638)** and Prestonfield (1687) – and their post-1840 'retro' imitators. However, some non-residential buildings in the area, e.g. Canongate Parish Church (1688–90; illus. p. 41), followed the same fashion. Isolated non-gentry examples from the eighteenth century exist in various parts of the country too, including

Above.
Earflap roof

Left.
Old Surgical
Hospital,
Edinburgh

East Kirk of
Rathen

Pilrig House

71 High Street in Dundee (c 1700),[52] **9 Boyndie Street in Banff (1740)** and the aptly named Dutch Gable House in Greenock (1755). Another 'Dutch' gable that actually looked Dutch adorned Aberdeenshire's Craigmyle House, built in 1676 and demolished in 1960 (illus. in my book

Lost Deeside, p. 203). As the inspiration for them came from Catholic, Calvinist and Episcopal Lutheran realms, some allies and some enemies, the curvilinear gables built by Scots are unlikely to have conveyed any overt message – unless it was 'I have travelled.'

4–6
Non-standard roofs 2: flat, or not quite?

Many Scottish buildings that aspire to grandeur, particularly from the eighteenth century, appear to have flat roofs from the

9 Boyndie Street, Banff

ground, either because their roofs really are flat, or more likely, that their shallow, usually 'hipped' roofs (see previous section) are hidden by a balustrade, or by a crenellated or non-crenellated parapet. Whether the roof really is flat is not especially significant, but the appearance of flatness is an important mark of Anglo-Italian grandiosity (see section 3–2, 'Marks of quality that transcend period', above). This look was popularised especially by Scottish architect Colen Campbell's book *Vitruvius Britannicus* (1715), and applied by William Adam to **Hopetoun House** soon after that. Having been worked on in turns by three of Scotland's most notable architects – Sir William Bruce, William Adam and Robert Adam – over a period of sixty years, Hopetoun is to some extent the gold standard of the eighteenth-century 'palace' style in Scotland, and the main basis of many **nineteenth-century urban and commercial copies**.

Especially after 1750, an otherwise flat or flat-looking roof was often combined with one or more classical pediments (see next section) as the 'Chinese whispers' Neo-Classicism of Bruce and the elder Adam gave way to the

Hopetoun House

The Edinburgh
GPO building of
1861, now known
as Waverley Gate

more severe and bookish Neo-Classicism of Adam's three
sons and others, including especially Robert Adam's chief
rival, Sir William Chambers. After their deaths – Chambers
and all three Adam brothers passed on in the 1790s – Scottish Neo-Classicism shifted in an even more severe and
theory-bound direction, usually dignified with the name
Greek Revival. This was epitomised by the **National Monument** (1817–22) to the fallen of the Napoleonic Wars which,
if funds had ever been found for its completion, would

The National
Monument

have been an exact replica of the Parthenon in Athens.

Genuinely flat roofs were also a signature feature of the Art Deco style of 1920–40, for which see sections 2–6 and 3–2, above.

4–7
Non-standard roofs 3: pediments, domes, spires and clock-towers

The bold, theatrical southern European Baroque style of the mid/late seventeenth century was briefly and belatedly popular in England, with examples including St Paul's Cathedral (1675–1711), the Royal Hospital, Chelsea (1681–89), Castle Howard (1699–1712) and Blenheim Palace (1705–24). Castle Howard in particular was influenced by the publications of Scottish architect Colen Campbell. But in Scotland itself prior to the nineteenth century, Catholicism was viewed with even greater suspicion than it was in England, and this almost papal style never really caught on. Victorian retro aside, William Adam's **Duff House** in Banff, completed 1739, is our only really significant example. The keynote of the Baroque style is the use of the details of ancient Roman architecture – including especially domes, classical pediments and columns – in new, 'busier' arrangements. The country's greatest retro-Baroque buildings can mostly be seen in Glasgow's late nineteenth-century Merchant Quarter, with the 1880s City Chambers in George Square probably being the finest of all.

It is not always possible, or indeed necessary, to separate the Baroque from the 'Palladian' style, as both often feature – at roofline level – stone urns, balustrades and shallow classical pediments. Since both styles aim at grandeur above all, you will not find a Baroque or Palladian cottage, gaol or country inn. However, not all buildings with classical pediments are in either of these palatial styles. In Scotland, especially after 1725, nearly any building – with or without a flat roof, balustrade, urns, etc – might be given a pediment. Scottish pediments dating from the second quarter of the eighteenth century are distinguished from both earlier and later ones by their height: having a top angle nearer to 100 degrees than to the 120–140 degrees preferred by the ancient Romans themselves (and by a later generation of more

What might have been

Had it been built to this 1791 design by Robert Adam, St George's Church in Charlotte Square, Edinburgh, would have been eighteenth-century Scotland's finest Baroque building, or at any rate its most typically Baroque one.

Pediment evolution, 1660–1840

Clockwise from top left: Classical pediments as differently used in the Palladian/Baroque, William Adam, Robert Adam and Greek Revival styles of the late seventeenth, early eighteenth, late eighteenth and early nineteenth centuries, respectively. Prior to the 1600s, pediments were barely seen in Scotland at all.

bookish architects exemplified by Sir William Chambers). Confronted by a building with one or more of these very tall, un-Roman-looking pediments – e.g. top right, above, and pp. 43 and 84 – you are actually fairly safe to assume a date of *c*. 1735 unless and until other features of the building steer you in some other direction. Scotland's flatter post-1750 pediments are also more likely than their immediate predecessors to contain coats of arms or sculptured figures, the older ones tending to be plain, or perhaps with a small round window in the middle.

Left.
Brechin Cathedral,
with the 11th-
century tower,
far right

Right.
King's College
Chapel, Aberdeen

Free-standing early medieval church towers of the tall, thin, round type commonly seen in Ireland were also built in Scotland, with two from the eleventh century surviving: one at Brechin and the other at Abernethy. The fifteenth century saw a fashion for pointed octagonal spires rising from battlemented square towers; these featured on some of the grandest Scottish churches, including St Machar's Cathedral, Aberdeen, which has two; **Brechin Cathedral**; Dunblane Cathedral; Corstorphine Church; and St Salvator's and Holy Trinity, both in St Andrews. So popular were octagonal stone spires in the fifteenth century that they were often added to much older buildings, e.g. the (non-battlemented) Restenneth Priory in Angus. Eastbank Church in Glasgow, however, is an early twentieth-century replica, distinguished as such by its extensive use of 'kneelers' (pp. 60–61), which were then at their height of popularity.

The considerably more intricate 'crown' or 'lantern' spires of **King's College Chapel in Aberdeen** and St Giles's Cathedral, Edinburgh (both *c.* 1500) are often thought to be distinctively Scottish. However, the very similar upper portion of the Market Cross of Chichester, West Sussex is the same age, while the lantern spire of the Cathedral of St Nicholas in Newcastle-upon-Tyne is half a century older than any similar structure north of the border. The 'lantern-esque' aluminium spire of St Michael's parish church, Linlithgow, is a 1964 homage to a lost 1480s original,[53] while lantern-spired Peebles Parish Church is a 'retro' structure of the mid 1880s.

The new Protestant Church's monetary poverty (compared with its Catholic predecessor) and its theological stance against ornamentation went hand in glove; and so it should not surprise us that a great many Scottish parish churches of the late sixteenth and seventeenth centuries were despised as **'barn-looking'**[54] and indeed constructed very much like barns, on a single level with few windows, and no separate bell-tower or steeple at all. Perhaps because

A 16th-century parish church of the type despised as 'barn-looking' by ministers of the Georgian age

St Tarquin's
Church, Fordyce

the wealth exhibited by the larger churches and abbeys had been the target of so much Reformation ire, steeples came back to Scottish religious life only very slowly. The majority that can be seen today are in fact from 1750–1840. Small village churches from before the eighteenth century are likely to have just a short belfry, often with the bell clearly showing. Larger parish churches of the turbulent seventeenth century, such as the *c.* 1600 parish church of Cockburnspath in Berwickshire, Old St Peter's in Peterhead (1647), and **St Tarquin's, Fordyce (1661)**, were sometimes built with tall-ish bell towers that were presumably handy for keeping the silver out of the hands of raiders. However, these towers usually had plain peaked roofs not unlike those of private houses of the same era: a far cry indeed from the battlements and dormer-covered octagonal spires of two centuries earlier.[55] Knightswood St Margaret's Parish Church in Glasgow is a fine late-1920s copy of this plain-peaked seventeenth-century style, by architect Sir Robert Lorimer.

Robert Gordon's Hospital

In the event, the post-Reformation resurgence of spires and clock towers came first to non-religious public buildings. Prior to the second quarter of the eighteenth century, many civic buildings did have steeples (e.g. the town halls a.k.a. 'tolbooths' of Culross, Musselburgh, New Aberdeen, Kirkcudbright and Crail), and these tended to be square, with conical or 'ogee' roofs. After 1725, the fashion shifted to octagonal towers, such as at **Robert Gordon's Hospital, Aberdeen (1731–39)**, Sanquhar Tolbooth (1735–37), Lochmaben Town Hall (1743–45), and the James VI Hospital in Perth (1748–52), as well as a select few well-architected religious structures of the same age, such as Donibristle Chapel in Dalgety Bay (1729–32). However, square towers with 'ogee' roofs continued to be made for civic purposes: as for instance on the charming Town House of Kintore (1737–47; illus. p. 169).

Scotland's first purpose-built Presbyterian church, St Columba's in Burntisland (1589–1600), originally had a wooden steeple of unknown size and shape; but it was only

Irvine Old Parish
Church

after 1750 that large numbers of Scottish parish churches rejoined the steeple-building movement. Ironically, this was often via direct imitation of Anglican churches built in London by Scottish Catholic expatriate James Gibbs. Examples of this adoption of Scottish-architected English church designs – all incorporating clocks – include Wellpark Mid Kirk, Greenock (1755); **Irvine Old Parish Church** (1774); and St Andrew's Parish Church, Dundee (1774–77). However, non-Gibbsian churches such as Mearns Parish Church (1755) also acquired clocks at this time. These are as good examples as any of the eighteenth century's Scottish-led unification of Britain's hitherto more diverse architectural styles (see section 2–3, above).

Wall-sundials were commonly seen on public buildings and the houses of the gentry before 1750, but these were generally *not* superseded by mechanical clocks in the case of houses; only town halls, schools, churches, etc. For the gentry, timekeeping did shift steadily to mechanical clocks after 1660, but to types carried on the person, or in carriages and sedan-chairs, or displayed inside the home. The mechanical clock now adorning the exterior of Crathes Castle (1596) is somewhat anomalous and was probably added after 1845, when R.W. Billings published a very detailed picture of the castle without one. 'Retro' replication of wall-sundials remains, for the time being, fairly uncommon. Fortunately, we have also largely avoided the practice of plugging up round windows with mechanical clocks, as the Dutch have chosen to do at the Palace of Het Loo.

4–8
Non-standard roofs 4: turrets and 'turrets'

As you will have noticed by now, I am not given to long passages of instruction in correct architectural jargon. However, the upper walls of hundreds of pre-1660 and post-1840 Scottish buildings boast an array of defensive and mock-defensive features that repay careful examination and categorisation.

In common parlance, 'turret' is bandied around a great deal, and might be used to mean nearly anything at roof level that gives off a vaguely medieval flavour – or even a massive round tower (with or without crenellations) that stretches all the way to the ground. In fact, though this can be somewhat subjective, a turret must be smaller than a tower, since its name – from the Italian *torretta* – actually means 'little tower'. This 'littleness' is a matter of both height and width. In terms of height, though a turret is often the part of a building that is highest above the ground, it is *not* conceived of as extending down to the ground, even if it is flush with the wall face. In terms of width, if you think a structure could contain no more than three adults standing abreast, and perhaps only one or two, it is better to call it a turret; while if you feel it could easily hold

A typical bartizan

four abreast or more, it is probably best to call it a tower. Further to this, an entire building can be said to consist of nothing but a tower (e.g. Liberton, p. 15), whereas a turret is only ever a small part of a larger whole.

Scotland's most common type of turret is further describable as a **bartizan**. These are always located on a corner or angle, and are never flush with the wall, but hang out beyond it, usually supported by corbels (see section 4–18, below). They are small: most are one storey or less in height, and appear large enough to contain only one person – probably seated. However, **multi-storey bartizans** do exist, most famously at Craigievar. Bartizans may or may not have roofs; on those that do, these are usually cone-shaped, pyramidal, or 'ogee' types suitable to structures of small diameter.

Like 'turret', the term 'cap-house' is rather broad and vague. There are two major types. The small or stair cap-house is similar to a bartizan in size and shape, but does not overhang the wall because its function is not as an observation post, but to provide protection from the weather for a stairway leading up onto a roof. As such, it is usually windowless; and no small- to medium-sized structure is likely to have more than one or two. The great cap-house, often merely called a cap-house, is fundamentally different: being an inhabitable structure, remarkably similar to village houses of a later era, often with multiple large windows, a pitched roof, and chimneys at each end. Most of these are one storey in height, but some are taller (e.g. at Towie Barclay Castle in Aberdeenshire) and others are of some-

what less than a full storey. The now-vanished late sixteenth century tower-house complex at Friars' Carse in Dumfriesshire, illus. p. 142, had a great cap-house at the centre of the tower with a stair cap-house immediately beside it. The same combination can still be seen on the roof of Sauchie Tower near Fishcross, Clackmannanshire.

Left.
A 2-storey bartizan, at Craigievar Castle

Right.
Round tower 'corbelled out' to a square shape, at Burleigh Castle

Great cap-houses always are situated within a parapet walkway, i.e., are quite visibly 'inboard' of the outer walls of the tower on which they sit. As such, they should not be confused with round towers that happen to be 'corbelled out' into a square house-like shape, as at **Burleigh Castle in Kinross (1582)**.

The liberal application of bartizans to nearly every size and type of building was the key, and in some cases the only, feature of the Scottish Baronial Revival style of 1840–1920. The other features mentioned in this section were also revived in the same period, but much less frequently.

Last days of a barmkin

Friars' Carse was an excellent example of a mid/late sixteenth century tower-house with a barmkin: a wall and outbuildings arranged to form a square-ish courtyard, used originally to protect livestock from raiders. It is notable that only two of the four buildings have slated roofs, the other two having thatch – despite being up to a century newer than the tower-house itself. The tiny, pointed structure on the right-hand side of the tower-house roof is called a stair cap-house and its function was to protect a stairwell from the elements. The house-like structure immediately to the stair cap-house's left, called a great cap-house, probably provided accommodation for the laird's immediate family. In the following century, however, such attic levels were more likely to house domestic servants, as we know was the case at Craigievar (completed 1626).

4–9
Dormers and 'headroom'

The point at which the edge of the roofing material meets the building's walls is known technically as the wall-head. Other than skylights (i.e. windows that lie flush with the roofing material at whatever angle), windows that are vertical and partly or entirely above the wall-head are known as 'dormers', regardless of their size or shape. Scottish buildings display an initially bewildering variety of dormers. Part of the confusion is that so many are post-1840 additions to Georgian- or pre-Georgian buildings; these latecomers are usually three- or five-sided and set well back from the wall-head.

Dormers that are round or oval (if viewed from directly above), each containing one standard sash window and

Dormers as misdirection

The typical and ubiquitous five-sided or 'bay-fronted' dormer windows of the 1840–1920 period are here seen atop a hotel built in 1670, originally as a coffee house, and otherwise reasonably original. This sort of modification has been carried out perhaps more often than not. As such, dormers of this type mean nothing other than that the building was still standing and inhabited at some time after 1840.

Edinburgh drum-shaped dormer of the later Georgian period

slated around the rest of their circumference, are very frequently seen on Edinburgh buildings from the end of the eighteenth century (see illus. of Thistle Court, p. 49). Prior to the 1760s, dormers had been out of fashion for a century, and in the pre-1660 period, they tended to be flush with the wall and protrude through it by approximately half their length. For a more complete discussion of pre-1660 dormers, see *Style 1540–1660*, above.

From 1840 to 1920, even as bay-fronted dormers were being stuck onto everything from renaissance castles forward, all previous dormer styles except the Jacobean 'cat-slide' were replicated endlessly, alongside several essentially new styles: some containing elaborate woodwork on either a 'Highland' or 'Tudor' theme (p. 55); some with crowsteps – rarely, if ever, a legitimate feature of dormers (as distinct from gables) in the era before 1750 when crowsteps were originally in vogue; and some with 'kneelers' (see p. 60–61).

Rarely, pre-1750 dormers sit directly on top of the wall-head, as at Dunstaffnage Castle

All of these changes in dormer styles between the mid sixteenth and mid twentieth centuries were coupled to changes in what might be called 'headroom': the distance

between the tops of a building's highest windows and the wall-head. Down to 1840, this is virtually a story of steadily increasing 'headroom'. Pre-1660 buildings tend to have 'negative headroom', insofar as almost all of them have dormers that break upward through the wall-head, or even sit on top of it as at **Dunstaffnage Castle.** From the 1660s down to the 1730s or '40s, many or most buildings (particularly the less expensive ones) tended to have *zero* 'headroom', with the top-most windows located at the top of the wall-head, flush with the roof – though this was also known in lairds' houses such as charming

Crowsteps on a dormer, especially such crisply cut ones, tend to mark it as Victorian.

Ardgrain (p. 000), built in several phases between 1664 and 1731. Nevertheless, the 1690s in particular saw a brief fashion for two-storey country- and village houses with the upper floor taller than the lower, e.g. Old Mains of Rattray in Perthshire (1694) and Borrowmeadow in Stirlingshire (*c.* 1700). Generally, the windows of such houses' upper floors were simply made taller than usual, but in some cases, a large amount of 'headroom' was left instead: as in the house of similar age shown at top right of p. 26.

In the middle years of the eighteenth century, a fashion for symmetrical window-surrounds (see section 3–2) necessitated that upper-floor windows be given some sort of decorative masonry border, which naturally included their top edges. Though the difference is subtle, 'zero headroom' *vs* fifteen inches of 'headroom' may be your first and best clue as to whether a relatively anonymous rural- or village building is from the reign of George I (1714–27) or George II (1727–60).

In and after the 1750s, ceilings became markedly higher in major public buildings and the dwellings of the well-to-do, and this led directly to unprecedentedly enormous amounts of 'headroom'. Though this affected Scottish society as a whole, it is especially noticeable in buildings by Sir William Chambers, James Craig (1739–95) and Robert Adam: for instance, **Chambers's 1772–74 town**

Extreme upper-floor headroom characterises this fine house built for Sir Laurence Dundas in the 1770s

house for Sir Laurence Dundas (now RBS) in St Andrew Square, Edinburgh; Craig's Physicians' Hall (1776; demolished 1844); and Adam's 1774–88 General Register House at the east end of Princes Street. These are extreme examples, however: on run-of-the-mill buildings of 1750–1840, 'headroom' is considerably less, with about one-third of window-height being typical, and 'zero-headroom' featuring in only the cheapest and least pretentious structures. Though 'zero headroom' never came back into vogue, 'negative-headroom' (in the form of pre-1660-style dormers) soon became fashionable as part of the post-1840 'retro' movement, especially between 1890 and 1940.

4–10
The normal Scottish window

The 'normal' Scottish window of the period 1680–1800 is a wooden sash-and-case design, usually with the wood painted white, in the overall form of a vertical rectangle.

It is usually two to five feet in height, and in width, something over half its height. It typically contains twelve panes – three across and four down. Each of the panes is in turn a vertical rectangle, though tending more toward squareness than the window it inhabits. Because these windows have been extensively retro-fitted to buildings from before 1680, and also continued to be used long after 1800, they may be deemed the normal windows for old Scottish buildings taken as a whole.

Like everything else, however, they evolved over time: with the wooden elements becoming ever thinner and more

Glazing-bar evolution

Typical sash-window glazing bars of the types popular c. 1680 (top) and c. 1820 (bottom), showing the decreasing thickness of the wooden elements over time, both in absolute terms and relative to the size of the glass pane. Plate glass – made by casting molten glass on an iron table-top and then hand-polishing both sides – was invented in France in 1688, and first made in Britain in 1773. But it was the application of steam power to the polishing phase, beginning in 1800, that first made it relatively affordable for windows. Thus, by the beginning of the Victorian period, it was suddenly possible to construct windows with many fewer distinct panes per square foot. The twelve-paned sash window with panes of less than one square foot apiece, which had been the norm for the previous century and a half, quickly fell from favour. By the 1840s–60s, large sash windows with just four panes were commonly seen. By the 1870s, windows with just two gigantic panes had been widely introduced, particularly – but not exclusively – in poorer urban districts.

delicate, and the glass area becoming bigger and bigger – in absolute terms as well as in relation to the wood. Put another way, original sash windows of the pre-1750 period have 'fatter' wooden elements than the inhabitants of later ages would tend to expect. After 1800, when steam power was first applied to window-glass making, larger panes became affordable, and thus the total number of panes could be reduced. By 1840, the norm was just four panes per window, and by 1870 just two per window, even as the windows themselves frequently attained heights of six feet and more.

The 'glazing bars', as the wooden pieces within the frame are known, grew steadily thinner over time, until by the second quarter of the nineteenth century they could seem like little more than lines on a vast glass surface. Thanks to better transport links and tax reductions in the first half of the nineteenth century, coal became widely affordable, and house-builders opted to admit more light via bigger windows, at the expense of energy efficiency, which was considered *passé*. As energy prices skyrocket, we should probably expect new houses to take on a pre-1750 appearance, at least as regards window size; the

Fewer, bigger panes

Curved or notched upper corners of the stone window-surround often accompany the two-paned and four-paned sash windows introduced in the Victorian era. This 'bottle-shaped' variety is usually from the 1870s, though we have seen dated examples from as early as 1863 and as late as 1890.

energy-efficient houses recently designed for the new towns of Knockroon in Ayrshire and Chapelton of Elsick, Aberdeenshire, are cases in point.

Perhaps in revolt against the over-simplification of traditional window design that was associated with cheap machine-made glass, Scotland's increasingly suburb-dwelling middle classes adopted a compromise: **sash windows with four, six, eight, nine, ten, or twelve panes on the top half, but only one or two panes on the bottom half.** These were especially popular from

1890–1910, to a point that they were sometimes inserted into buildings of earlier periods, especially in former rural villages that had 'suburbanised'.

Sash windows with a multi-panel top half and a single-panel bottom half were popular from 1890–1910. Like most pre-1920 building features, they have been extensively replicated in recent years

Scottish windows that are four panes wide and six or more panes deep, for instance at Holyrood Palace and the Gordon barracks in Bridge of Don, Aberdeen, frequently indicate a building that was not a private house, but in public ownership or intended for public use from the start.

All sash windows are not created equal, of course, and the post-1875 replacement of the many-paned by the two-paned variety in Edinburgh's City Chambers (built as the Royal Exchange, 1753–61; illus. p. 133, bottom right) make it look rather cheap and forlorn. Conversely, the bold use of more complicated sash windows can make far humbler structures look their very best, the garden pavilions of Pitmedden being a case in point.

Because glass is technically 'amorphous and non-crystalline' – essentially a very slow-moving liquid rather than a solid – original glass of more than about 100 years old is of a visibly wavy or blotchy appearance, even at a distance of twenty feet or more, and slightly thicker at the bottom than the top. Over an even longer period, a pane of glass will have flowed downward to the point that its top disconnects from its frame, and wind, water, and insects can get through. Tempered glass, invented after the First World War, slows this process but cannot prevent it.

Windows that appear under-sized relative to the size

Before sash windows were invented

Before sash windows, Scottish windows that were of glass at all (as opposed to just holes curtained off on the inside) had numerous tiny panes bound together with lead. Few such remain, and even reconstructions – as at Milne's Court, Edinburgh – are rarely seen; so this is now wrongly reckoned an 'English' or 'Tudor' style. No significant quantities of window glass were made in Great Britain before 1678, so it had to be imported by sea. The panes, or really fragments of glass, used to make windows in the mid 1670s and earlier might therefore be of various shapes, but all tended to be very small. Those with predominately diamond-shaped pieces were clearer and thus more expensive, and those with rounder pieces were more opaque/distorted and therefore cheaper.

The cheaper type of 'pre-sash' northern European window: detail from *The Ill-matched Couple* by Lucas Cranach the Elder, 1532

Square windowpanes, bound with lead, in a Jacobean merchant's house, Edinburgh

Non-portrait windows

'Landscape' windows and 'landscape' panes are usually a feature of Art Deco buildings from the Interwar years (1919–39), but occasionally you will see one or both in the attic or basement windows of Neo-Classical houses from the period 1750–1840. 'Landscape' windows also sometimes featured on the lowest floor of late sixteenth century tower-houses: see pp. 104 and 142. Tiny square windows set high up in gables, very near the edge, were a characteristic feature of Scottish houses from the 1660–1750 period, as seen on pp. 26 (right) and 111.

and age of the building may reflect an Irish influence (upon either the builders or the owners), in buildings of almost any age. This is particularly so on the West Coast. Occasionally my friends try to 'stump' me by asking me to identify a Scottish-looking house that is actually in some other country; if I feel the building is 'squinting' at me I will guess that it is actually in Ireland, and this often proves to be the case. The same trick attempted with Welsh, Cornish and Cumbrian buildings has the opposite result: in those places, house windows have generally been broader than Scottish windows of the same age and height.

4–11
Non-standard windows 1:
horizontal rectangles and squares

Despite the dominance of the vertical rectangle in all periods, many other window shapes have been used. Horizontal rectangles, a.k.a. 'landscape' format, are seen in some of the very finest Scottish buildings from before 1840, but only in the attic and/or basement levels and (after 1750) immediately over doors. A building whose windows are all horizontal rectangles is almost certainly from after World War One; and a building whose windows are all square, or a mixture of 'landscape' and square, is probably from after World War Two. This is an area where the present-day designers of high-end retro-Georgian houses (in England as well as in Scotland) often give their game away.

Shop window of the 1840–1920 period

That being said, square or 'landscape' non-opening windows with square panes, if located on the ground floor of an urban- or village high street building, may be **original shop or pub windows from the nineteenth century**. This diagnosis is even more likely to be correct if the windows in question are slightly convex, as seen here. Public buildings of various periods also often made use of perfectly square panes, albeit usually within vertical rectangular windows.

Windows inserted directly above exterior doors as a part of the doorway are called 'fanlights' if shaped like a fan (see pp. 50 and 151), or 'transom windows' if not.[56] Fanlights and other transom windows were introduced in Scotland

More, or less, authentic glazing

Though windows with (usually white-painted) wooden glazing
bars of a decidedly post-1660 appearance have often been
inserted into the openings at a later date (left), the square
or nearly square windows that were popular in the sixteenth
century would originally have contained leaded glass (right).

in the period 1750–1840 and have been popular ever since,
in part because the increased overall scale of buildings after
1750 would have made standard doors look too small in
comparison to the larger structures they now inhabited.
The 1730s former boys' school at 113 Mill Hill in Musselburgh (illus. p. 158)
contains a clumsy
Victorian attempt to
retro-fit a transom win-
dow into a doorway of
earlier/smaller propor-
tions, with the result
that tall visitors may
receive a nasty crack on
the head. Such is the
price of fashion.

A 'true' fanlight, in
that the fan design
determines its
overall shape

4–12
Non-standard windows 2: other shapes and materials

Small round or horizontal-oval windows called **'bullseyes'**, or even triangular windows, were often seen above the front doors of the first generation of unfortified Scottish country mansions in the 1660s-80s (see p. 44). **Round-topped rectangular windows** were initially meant to evoke Italy, and were strongly favoured by architect William Adam. Adam added them in the 1720s to Hopetoun House, which had originally been built with 'normal' windows by Sir William Bruce and Tobias Bauchope between 1699 and 1703.

William Adam also installed Scotland's first window in the round-topped **'Venetian' or 'Palladian' style** in the late 1720s at Drum House, Gilmerton, after which he continued to create non-'Venetian' but still round-topped windows, for instance at the House of Dun in Angus (1730), the Parish Church of Hamilton (1732), and his most important commission, Duff House in Banff (1735–39). By the end of the eighteenth century, perhaps as a result of this preference on the part of Scotland's 'most Scottish' architect,

Left.
A bullseye window of the mid Victorian period

Right.
A late Georgian round-topped rectangular window

An exceptionally ornate example of a Venetian window in East Lothian; compare p. 89

round-topped rectangular windows were simply a Scottish mark of cost and distinction, rather than of particular foreign influences (see also section 3–2, above).

By the 1860s, this sense of distinction had passed, and round-topped windows – albeit smaller and narrower ones than in William Adam's day – were simply in vogue for buildings of all sorts: from suburban villas to railway stations, pubs and banks. Around 1880 they went rather out of fashion again. After this date, round-topped windows – now really **half-round or semi-circular windows** – became a prominent marker of state schools, factories, power stations, town halls, and other large non-residential buildings deemed at the time to be of secondary aesthetic importance. The 1870s were a transitional period, during which the windows of many buildings – particularly those built in the then-popular 'French Gothic' or 'Addams Family' style (see also section 4–5, above) – had their top two corners 'cut off' (p. 145).

All round-topped window types must be carefully distinguished from **rectangular windows that are merely 'humped**

Toward the end of the Victorian era, immense semi-circular windows became a popular feature of schools, factories and power stations

This hump-topped window shape was popular in the first two decades of the 20th century

up' on top in a barely noticeable shallow curve. This style, though it was exceptionally popular for grand buildings in France and the Netherlands as early as the 1710s, was barely seen in Scotland before 1880; the great hall of Stirling Castle (1503), the now-derelict House of Gray near Dundee (1714–16) and the basement layer of W.H. Playfair's

Leopold Place, Edinburgh (1818–21) are rare exceptions proving the rule. Easy to achieve using brick, a material that was hardly seen in Scotland before Victorian times, this type of hump-topped window was at its most popular here from 1900–20. However, it should be noted that doors and archways in this shape – known technically and rather unmemorably as a 'segmental arch' – were built in Scotland in all periods.

Windows with pointed tops fall into two broad sub-categories: on the one hand, the **sharply pointed 'Gothic'** intended to evoke the pre-1500 European world in general, and religious building in particular; and on the other, the **shallow-pointed 'Tudor'** intended to evoke sixteenth-century England. In Scotland, which was never ruled by the Tudors, 'Tudor' windows – and doorways – are almost always from after 1750, and mostly from after 1840. The almost-'Tudor' windows of Sir William Chambers's famous Dunmore Pineapple (1761) are highly unusual for such an early date. A third type, **a simple pentagonal shape featuring no curves**

Left.
A rare use of Gothic-arched windows in a suburban house of the early to mid 19th century

Right.
The Tudor-arched windows of the Dunmore Pineapple (1761)

Rare five-sided window, c. 1900

at all, is also very occasionally spotted in buildings from the nineteenth century.

Gothic-pointed windows that are genuinely from the Middle Ages will likely be part of a clearly signposted Ancient Monument. Those that are not genuinely medieval are mostly from after 1800, and may indicate that the building has been owned by a church, and/or been worked on by architect William Burn. There is also a vague and possibly unprovable link between Gothic-pointed windows and Episcopalian owners, at least in the years 1800–30. A very unusual use of Gothic-pointed windows on a non-ecclesiastical Scottish building of the seventeenth century can be seen in Heriot's Hospital, Edinburgh (1628–42).

The first use of stained glass in Scottish dwellings, and its first reappearance in Scottish churches since the Reformation of the mid sixteenth century, both occurred as symptoms of 'retro' fever after 1840. The height of stained glass's popularity in domestic settings occurred from 1880 to 1910. In this, the city of Glasgow 'played a large and conspicuous role, producing between 1870 and 1914 some of the finest ecclesiastical and domestic stained glass in Europe'.[57] Notable Scottish makers included Ballantine & Allan (founded Edinburgh 1837), David Keir & Sons (Glasgow, 1847), Cottier's (Glasgow, 1867) and J. & W. Guthrie (Glasgow, 1884).

You will occasionally see windows that look vaguely like sash windows, but which are in fact made of painted metal rather than wood and open via side-hinges. These appear to have been sold in great quantity, particularly to farmers, over a relatively short period: roughly the 1930s.

4–13
False windows

The infamous Window Tax, introduced in 1696 in England and Wales, was in force in Scotland from 1748 to 1851. Though the Scottish version of the tax was shorter-lived than its southern neighbour, it affected more buildings: those with seven windows or more, as opposed to ten or more, as in England.[58] It led directly to three distinct phenomena: 1) existing windows being sealed up; 2) houses being built with fewer places for windows; and 3) houses being built with window apertures filled with masonry, but ready to be un-blocked when the tax was repealed, or if the owners' financial circumstances improved.

However, the importance of the Window Tax can be overplayed. Some windows were blocked for reasons other than tax, and some were made 'blind' from the outset for aesthetic reasons alone. My own house was built as a single-storey gate lodge about 1800. When it gained an upper storey in the 1840s, this necessitated the insertion of a stair-case, but the only logical place for it cut cleanly across an

Blocked window

existing window. **That window** was then filled in with stone, but is still clearly discernible from the outside. Given the large number of buildings that were likewise expanded upward over the course of the nineteenth century (see section 4–18, below), this was undoubtedly a common solution to a common problem. On the other side of Musselburgh, the early Georgian former school at 113 Mill Hill has obviously had a large and grand Venetian-style window blocked up, possibly as a result of similar considerations arising from its conversion into flats (p. 160).

Heavily modified

Built as a laird's town house in the 1730s and later used as a boys' school, this building in East Lothian (now flats) has been modified more than most. Colour and texture variations to the stonework of the end-gable indicate the position of a former 'Palladian' window, as well as a very different original roof angle and narrower chimney.

Windows that have been made and then blocked up – whether due to these sorts of conversion issues, or due to tax reasons – differ fundamentally from **'blind' windows**, which really are mere surface depressions, never intended to contain glass but rather to serve the Georgian era's obsession with symmetry (see especially section 3–3). Such schemes have often, but not always, been accompanied by the painting of false sash windows into the openings.

Left.
Blind windows

Right.
Four blind windows, faux-painted to appear as if they contain glass

4–14
Window pairs

This can initially be a rather tricky and subjective area: when can we be sure we are looking at a true *pair* of windows as opposed to two similar windows that happen to be close together? Without advocating that you go around sizing up other people's houses with a tape measure, I would suggest that if a window is truly a member of a pair or trio, it will be separated from its mate(s) by no more than one foot of masonry, and usually only five to ten inches, almost always in the form of a distinct, one-piece vertical stone bar.

Systematic window-pairing came into vogue in Scotland with spectacular suddenness and force in the mid Victorian era.

Systematic window-pairing

One of the most widespread and telling features of Scottish architecture of the period 1880–1910 is the use of pairs (or threes) of identical windows separated only by a thin bar of stone, five to ten inches in width. This separating bar can be very ornate or very plain or anything in between – this one is above average – but its presence is a strong indication that the building originated in this fairly brief period. This '1820' building is actually from after 1880, as its paired, two-paned sash windows strongly suggest: a further reminder that you should never trust a date-stone.

The mere handful of surviving forerunners of this look – which was conceivably intended to be Neo-Romanesque (see section 2–1) – include the 1503 great hall of Stirling Castle; Lamb's House in Leith (1587); and the 1589–1600 parish church of Burntisland in Fife.[59] Its use within the mock-castle style of the late Georgian period also occurred, but again, only very rarely.

In any case, window-pairing was clearly accepted as 'traditional' by the 1880s – perhaps because the leading retro-Baronial architect of the previous three decades, David Bryce, had used window-pairs on the Old Surgical Hospital, Edinburgh.[60] Pairing also allowed terraced- and semi-detached houses – both new inventions of the 1750–1840 period – to share dormer windows with their neighbours (though this was done only sometimes). At a rough guess, paired windows adorn an absolute majority of the residential and small commercial buildings built in south-eastern and central Scotland between 1880 and 1940, including even low-rise blocks of council flats. Be cautious, however, about assigning a post-1880 date to a building that has only one window-pair. The fashion for these was strong enough that they were occasionally 'punched through' an older building, as a fairly reliable means of adding light without significantly decreasing the wall's structural integrity. So in this, as in all cases, window evidence must be combined with door, chimney, roofline, masonry and other available evidence before any firm conclusions are drawn. Likewise, pairs or trios of narrow round-topped rectangular windows may date from the general craze for narrow round-topped windows in the 1860s and '70s (see previous section), which the stylistically precocious

False positive: these 18th-century windows just happen to be close together

William Burn had used in Inverness Castle as early as 1836. A few Bryce buildings other than the Old Surgical Hospital – including Balfour Castle in the Orkneys – also incorporated one or more window pairs. Bryce died in 1876.

One further point of caution: the typical flat-topped post-1880 double window should not be confused with **windows in eighteenth-century or older commercial buildings** that simply happen to be quite close together.

4–15
Window trios

Trios of windows, though they were almost as popular as paired windows between 1890 and 1910, have a somewhat more complex history. They evolved from the 'Venetian' or 'Palladian' window: itself a type of triple window in which the middle window of the three is taller and wider than the other two, and rounded on the top (pp. 89 and 155). Though 'Venetians' have been used sporadically in Scotland ever since the late 1720s, by the end of the eighteenth century there had arisen a **degenerate version** in which the middle window was still taller and wider than its fellows, but not rounded on top (e.g. on the third floor of Culzean Castle, 1777–92).

A degenerate, square-topped version of a Venetian window

This being aesthetically displeasing, the next step was to reduce the height of the middle window to the same height as those flanking it. The very first occurrences of **this new arrangement** may have been as early as 1780; and Robert Adam, who died in 1792, is credited with several. But it was between 1800 and 1840 that these triple windows became hugely popular, especially for middle-class residential buildings. Usually, the two flanking windows are one pane wide and four panes high, with the middle window being the 'normal' Scottish sash window of three panes wide by four high. I would even go so far as to say that this is one of the very few indicators of a distinctively Scottish Regency style,[61] the existence of which was once famously questioned by leading architectural historian Sir Niklaus Pevsner. Sporadic 'retro' replication of the Scottish Regency triple window began as early as 1870, and has never entirely stopped. However, most of the examples you see (and nearly all examples with four-paned side windows) will be from 1815, give or take fifteen years. A version with wooden rather than stone vertical separators was seen in the late Regency period, e.g. in **these** very attractive *c.* 1820 semi-detached houses at 3–4 Grove Street, Musselburgh.

The Scottish Regency window-trio is easily distinguishable from the popular window-trio of 1890–1910, because

Window trios: Regency vs Victorian

The characteristic triple windows of 1800–40 (left) compared against those of 1890–1910 (right). Though trios with a wider window in the middle continued to be made in the period 1840–1920, the difference in width was never as stark. As with everything else, considerably more accurate 'retro' copies of the original look appeared after 1920, albeit only rarely.

in the latter period, each of the three windows in a trio is of exactly the same size as the others.

Though the great majority of bay windows are trios of a sort, some are quads or even sextets, and so they will be considered in their own section, below.

4–16
Bay windows and bay-fronted dormers

A bay window – technically an *oriel*, pronounced oriole, if its base doesn't meet the ground – is one that protrudes beyond the main footprint of the building, in approximately a half-hexagon shape (if viewed from directly above). It presumably evolved from crude, square oriels of the mid sixteenth century, as can be seen at Hallbar Tower in South Lanarkshire. Very elaborate bay windows of the familiar half-hexagonal type enjoyed a brief vogue in Scotland in the first quarter of the seventeenth century, appearing on two of the grandest houses in the kingdom: Huntly Castle in Aberdeenshire (1605) – the most expensive house of its generation – and Pinkie House in Musselburgh (1613), built for Alexander Seton, a powerful politician and leading

Bay window origins

The typical post-1840 bay window is a greatly simplified revival of this early-seventeenth-century style, seen here on Maybole Castle in Carrick.

patron of architecture. But these pre-1660 examples were rarities even in their own time, and in the eighteenth century's great age of flat surfaces and symmetry, none seem to have been built in Scotland at all.

The bay window's revival, amounting almost to total reinvention, was a late (post-1810) development within the charming mock-castle movement in architecture that had taken off around 1770 (see section 4–3, above). From this fashionable base, the bay window quickly became a commonplace feature of both suburban residential and urban mixed commercial/residential buildings, of varying quality. By and large, the high-end, pre-1860 Scottish bay window can be distinguished from its inexpensive and anonymous successors of 1860 to the present, in that the latter are narrower and deeper, i.e., all three sides of the bay are identical in width; or at any rate, the middle window

Bay window revival

The wide, shallow, ornate bay windows that became fashionable in the first half of the nineteenth century, exemplified here by Lady Glenorchy's Church (1846; now the Glasshouse Hotel) were modelled on those of Pinkie House (1613) and other Jacobean mansions of the highest rank. Between these dates, however, almost no use of bay windows occurred at all, and – bay-fronted dormers aside – even retrospective additions of bays to buildings from 1660 to 1840 have been mercifully few.

The half-hexagon shape of many new toll-takers' cottages of the early 1800s may have fed the bay-window craze

is no more than twice as wide as the other two.

The older bays, whether good Regency copies or 1600s originals, can have fronts that are up to four times wider than their sides. That being said, the magnificent oriels of Huntly Castle and its near-contemporary, Maybole Castle in Ayrshire, do have sides of equal length. Fortunately, the odds that you will ever need to date a whole building based on its bay window(s) alone are very slim.

A potential for confusion exists in the proliferation of **toll-takers' cottages** from the first decades of the nineteenth century, many of which were built in a half-round, half-hexagon or half-octagon shape with numerous windows to facilitate the observation of travellers on the road. Mostly, these are still located on important roads, and are of one storey, plain and well-built. Conceivably, the sudden arrival *c.* 1798 of these curious semi-public structures fed in to the nineteenth-century's bay-window craze.

The new, mass-market bay windows of 1840–1920 included that great pitfall, the **bay-fronted dormer** (see also p. 143), which seems intended to make all Scottish buildings look as similar as possible. When reading a building, block them from view with your hand if necessary. Nothing

Bay-fronted
dormers

screams 'afterthought!' like a bay-fronted dormer. If every one of them turned into a solar panel tomorrow, the country would be a great deal richer – and not just financially.

If you are sure that a building is from the eighteenth century, except for the fact that it has a bay window, you should proceed from the hypothesis that the said window was added later. This is not, after all, an especially difficult building operation, though fortunately it has been done much less frequently than the tacking-on of dormers.

4–17
Doors, doorways and archways

Yetts, as defensive iron grilles over doors were known, were outlawed in 1606. However, they continued to be fitted (or put back on, due to civil warfare) as late as the 1650s in some remoter areas. Doors themselves were, before 1660, often covered by several dozen metal studs; many also had a face-sized observation hatch at face height, which in turn might be covered by a metal grille. Some such doors survive, and others have been realistically re-created. Though most Scottish doors were square-topped in all periods, a substantial minority of pre-1660 doors (e.g. at Craigievar) were of the 'hump-topped' shape known technically as a segmental arch. This is somewhat odd since, as we have seen, hump-topped *windows* were all but unheard of before the nineteenth century, and at their most popular from 1900 to 1920. Pends (see section 2–2) were also likely to be hump-topped – even in periods when gates in boundary walls were usually round-topped or square, and when hump-topped windows were as yet virtually unknown.

Particularly before 1750, as with window-surrounds, the width and complexity of a door's surrounding stone carving (if any) was positively correlated with the social status of the owner, even though the doors themselves tended to be more or less uniformly small for all classes. As we have seen, there was a quantum leap in ceiling height and therefore door height after 1750 which led directly to the first use of transom windows (sections 2–4 and 4–11 above). Door-knockers are also mostly from 1750 and after.

Yett

It was in the 1750–1840 period that double doors became commonplace on residential buildings and shops, though they were never the majority. To the dismay of large modern persons carrying large modern luggage, many Scottish residential double doors – though kept firmly locked on one side or the other – are only fractionally wider than single doors of the same age. As such, unusually wide double doors on an otherwise house-like building could indicate its former status as a chapel, school, public hall or other structure that large numbers of people were expected to enter simultaneously.

Aristocratic buildings of 1660–1750 were often fitted with the modern type of doors, i.e. with recessed square and/or rectangular panels surrounded by hemispherical mouldings. Humbler buildings' doors of the same period

– no longer being fitted with metal studs, grilles and hatches – tended to be severely plain. After 1750, however, the panel-and-moulding type of door became general in urban areas, as well as on middle-class buildings of the countryside such as farmhouses and manses. Stained glass windows set into doors, and domestic stained glass generally, are post-1840 phenomena and were at their most popular from 1880 to the outbreak of the First World War. Clear glass windows within doors (as distinct from transom windows) are usually from the twentieth century, and sometimes a replacement for stained glass. All this being said, however, doors of all sorts have been so frequently replaced with 'up to date' models that they are not really a primary marker of anything.

Prior to their being taken up by the gentry in the later seventeenth century, entrance doors more than half a storey above ground level – whether reached by steps or ladders – continued to indicate a commercial, probably industrial, function. Even after 1660, however, and into the twentieth century, a door on an upper floor not accessible by stairs, i.e. with a sheer drop to the ground, was associated with industry and agriculture.

The presence of multiple doors on the entrance front (pp. 45, 46, 129 and 171) is another fairly good sign that a building from before 1750 was built not as a house but for commerce or administration. This distinction was blurred or eliminated in the period 1750–1840, however, due largely to the invention of semi-detached and terraced houses. Debates rage about who invented the semi-detached house, with claims being made for Richard Gillow (Lancaster, 1758), Gayfere & Groves (Blackheath, London 1776) and Michael Searles (Kennington, London c. 1792). It is interesting that, though Scotsmen dominated the field of architecture in Britain as a whole during the eighteenth century (section 2–3), the debate on the origin of the 'semi' has not hitherto touched either upon Scottish buildings or designers. In my opinion, the oldest examples of semi-detached houses in Scotland are the two pairs collectively known as Thistle Court, located at 1–4 Thistle Street in Edinburgh New Town (illus. p. 49), whose construction began in 1767.

With regard to subdivided buildings generally, it is worth noting that Scotland's population density today is just 174 people per square mile (England surpassed this figure in the year 1811, and today has 1,054 people per square mile). Indeed, space has never really been at a premium here,

Special features of small civic buildings

The Town House of Kintore (1737–47) is marked out as non-residential by its clock tower and proliferation of doors; remove these features and it might easily be a laird's country house of the same age. A very similar arrangement of doors and stairs was found in the now-demolished Customs House of Dunbar, built in 1710, and other examples could no doubt be traced.

Blocked archways (left) should be distiguished from mere arch-shaped depressions (right) that were popular for stylistic reasons

except in the great fortress-towns of Edinburgh and Stirling. Just 14 per cent of Scottish rural buildings from before the First World War are of three storeys or more, with some parishes having none at all. That being said, blocks of flats of six to eight storeys – commonplace by the late seventeenth century in Edinburgh – were unknown until a much later date in England, and even in the north of Scotland. Accordingly, visitors from Manchester or Aberdeen should not be too quick to dismiss the towering 'tenements' of Edinburgh as 'too tall to be old'; in fact, a great many from the eighteenth century, and a few from earlier, are still standing and in regular use. Nevertheless, even these mighty edifices usually made do with one front door and one back door.

The town house (i.e. town hall) of Kintore, Aberdeenshire, completed in 1747, can be distinguished from a gentleman's house of the same age not only by its clock tower but by its proliferation of doors, including one on the first floor, accessed by steps. This concept is also found in the Tolbooth of Musselburgh (sixteenth century with eighteenth-century additions).

Unlike false windows, which as we have seen were often added for the sake of symmetry, most blocked-up entrances to Scottish buildings – and there are a very great many – actually used to be doorways or gateways. However, **blocked archways** should be carefully distinguished from mere **arch-shaped depressions** that were popular for stylistic reasons from 1750–1840, as well as from arched bracing intended to add strength to a wall, without ever having been part of an entrance. The latter can often be recognised by its extreme height above the ground level, e.g. in our picture of Lauriston Castle on p. 104.

4–18
Walls 1: string courses and corbelling

'String course' and 'band course' are both technical terms for any broadly horizontal line of stones or bricks, one stone or brick in height, that stands proud of the rest of the building's surface – often poking through the harling, in the case of a building that has been harled. Such a feature is more likely to be described as a 'string course' if slightly squiggly in appearance, and as a **'band course'** if truly horizontal, though the terms remain interchangeable. During the retro fever of 1840–1920 string courses were sometimes applied simply to achieve a 'look': specifically, the look of fortified houses of the 1540–1660 period such as Crathes (1553–96) and Tolquhon (1584–89), whose string courses at their best – particularly **where they change height/direction to merge with heraldry frames** (section 3–1 above) – might be counted as sculptural works of art. However, on many buildings of all periods, string courses were used to conceal – and therefore potentially to announce – that a

building has been extended upwards. My own house has a prominent band course separating the regular masonry of its Georgian ground floor from the intentionally irregular masonry of the upper floor that was added in early Victorian times. This practice was even more common in the case of shops than houses (see section 4–4 above).

String or band courses should not automatically be assumed to hide an upward extension, however. They were applied to numerous structures from all periods simply for decoration, albeit usually still marking the approximate level of a floor. Neither should they be confused with **corbelling**: a line of stones that supports a wider wall above. Though often misdescribed as having a 'string course', Craigievar's beautiful

Above.
Band course marking the addition of a third level to a small commercial building

Right.
Crathes Castle, string course detail

Craigievar Castle,
corbelling detail

squiggly line (concealing/announcing that it is a 1620s
upward extension of a tower begun and abandoned before
1611) in fact consists of corbelling, since everything above
it is wider than everything below. Over-enthusiastic use of
corbelling may indicate that an entire tower-house is a post-
1840 copy, as at Dall House in Highland Perthshire (1854–
55), which has five courses of corbelling, in contrast to the
one, two or three courses that were normal in the early
seventeenth century.

4–19
Walls 2: walls that lean or curve

Occasionally, particularly in rural villages and small ports,
we see small houses whose walls appear to lean backwards
or inwards. The point at which their walls meet the ground
or pavement is thick and 'blobby'. This is often a sign of
archaic construction techniques involving boulders and/or
clay; the use of both together is
known as '**clay bool**'. Many such
houses were built before 1750,
when clay was still a normal
construction material, and the use
of larger stones closer to the ground
and smaller ones nearer the roof
was also usual (see next section).
But with this as with all other wall-
making techniques, once it was

An uneven
foundation may
be evidence of
clay bool
construction

Intentionally
inward-leaning
walls in a Greek
Revival building
of the 1850s

invented, someone, somewhere continued to use it for decades, whether due to cost considerations or their own skill-set or mere aesthetic preferences. Alternating courses of stone and turf were also frequently seen in small rural buildings of the seventeenth century, one of which survives at Langholm, Dumfriesshire. This technique, too, could lead to a wall that appears to lean inward, since the foundation of such a building was always of (large) stones, not turf. If a wall is leaning forward/ outward at the top, however, this may be a sign of shoddy construction practices or internal damage; do not stand too close for too long.

Between 1700 and 1800, cottages changed from oval to rigidly rectangular plans, via this transitional type with rounded corners

Of course, none of this should be confused with carefully crafted buildings, particularly in the Greek Revival style of the early/mid nineteenth century, some of whose exterior walls **slope inward as an intended element of the design**.

Considered from above, many grand Scottish buildings of all periods have walls that curve in the obvious forms of towers, stair-towers, domes, turrets and so forth. However, some humble one-storey cottages – though broadly rectangular – also have markedly curved corners at one or both ends. Many of **these, some with traditional thatched roofs,** can be seen in the Hebrides. It is unclear if this type of house was always more prevalent in the islands, or simply more likely to survive there than on the mainland. Architectural historians of the north-east Scottish mainland believe that the curve-cornered cottages reflect a gradual evolution from the actually round or oval huts depicted in the late seventeenth century engravings of John Slezer, and the truly rectangular 'but-and-ben' cottages of the nineteenth century. If this is the case, then cottages with four curved corners are likely to be from the first half of the eighteenth century and those with only two curved corners from the second half. The toll-takers' cottages built between 1798 and 1858 (see also section 4–16 above) sometimes had their 'observation' ends constructed in a half-circular rather than half-hexagonal form, while doocots (section 3–4) are round more often than not.

The idea that a whole street of houses could be designed and built in a unified, majestic curve was pioneered in Bath in the 1750s, and the builders of Edinburgh New Town copied this in several places.

4–20
Walls 3: materials, colours and textures

Most old Scottish buildings that are still standing were built of stone, or else mainly of stone with some brick or un-fired clay elements. While it might seem of fundamental importance in reading a building, the type of stone used is seldom more than a function of where the building is – a fact which, as mentioned in the introduction, the observant traveller will already know. Most Edinburgh buildings are of grey sandstone, and most Aberdeen buildings are of grey granite; lumpy red 'puddingstone' is the norm in Callander, pink and buff sandstone in Dundee, and so forth. Scotland has generally been a net exporter of building materials other than wood (which frequently was imported from Scandinavia even in pre-industrial times). Aberdeen granite – and the men who knew how to work it – appeared throughout Britain's nineteenth-century empire, and other countries besides. Sadly, though the supply is very far from exhausted, labour-cost differences and environmental short-sightedness now make it more economical to import Chinese granite for Aberdeenshire house-building than to quarry stone locally.

Though wood has been used as a building material in Scotland since prehistoric times, and bricks have been manufactured here since the late Stuart period, all-brick and all-wood structures have been, and remain, uncommon. In 1827, surviving timber buildings were condemned as 'the wreck and rubbish of past centuries, sinking fast under

Half-brick Georgian house in Old Aberdeen: one of a handful of places in Scotland where bricks were made at such an early date

the pressure of their own weight, receptacles of filth and hotbeds of contagion'.[62] Bricks were made and extensively used in Old Aberdeen and Laurencekirk in the eighteenth century. They were also frequently deployed at Errol in Perthshire as early as 1710, probably as a straight substitute for un-fired clay. The size of Scottish bricks became much larger than the previous, and modern, norm for some years after 1784, when a poorly thought-out per-brick tax led manufacturers to make their product as large as possible. Bricks from the last years of the eighteenth century – unless imported – therefore tend to be a foot long and up to four inches thick. But as a rough rule of thumb, outside the three communities mentioned above, a building will date from after 1840 if its visible exterior contains more than 50 per cent brick,[63] 30 per cent iron/steel, 20 per cent glossy tile, or (doors and windows aside) 20 per cent wood, whether alone or in any combination. Provided that a building is made of the same stuff as the majority of the buildings in the surrounding area – inevitably stone – one need not infer anything more than that a quarry of that type of stone is, or was, located nearby. But by the same token, a building that stands out dramatically from its immediate neighbours, in terms of its basic building material, may have other things that are special about it, too, and may well repay a bit of extra investigation.

Many Scottish walls, whether part of a building or free-standing, have a small red rectangular Royal Mail post-box mortared directly into them. These post-boxes themselves are all from after 1856. They are marked with the reigning sovereign's monogram, i.e. 'VR' to 1901, 'E VII R' 1901–11, 'GR' 1911–36, 'G VI R' 1937–52, and 'E II R' from 1952 onward; but this is not to suggest that any were replaced simply because the sovereign changed. While a post-box of any age might have been inserted into a wall of any equal or greater age, the converse is not true: a VR post-box should not generally be found in a wall built after 1901, or a 'GR' postbox in a wall built after 1936, etc. This makes them a reasonable confirmation check on the age of particular streets.

When confronted with a stone wall that is neither harled nor thickly painted, one can judge its stonework in five major dimensions. These are:

- Surface texture of the stones used
- Size of the stones used, and the uniformity of their size
- Colours of the stones used, and the uniformity of their colours
- Outer shapes of the stones used, and the uniformity of their shapes
- Arrangement of the stones used

1. *Surface texture of the stones used*. Well into the nine-teenth century, local masons using simple hand tools did the best they could to make the 'public faces' of the buildings they worked on as smooth as their time,

budgets and technology allowed. Much of the great charm of pre-Victorian buildings is the resultant surface quality, which can be described as almost, but not quite, even. **Tool marks** are often clearly visible as a 'stippling' effect, frequently varying in direction from one stone to another. Subsequent generations, particularly in the 1890s, tried and failed to replicate this mechanically, yielding a Mars-like surface of jagged, mountainous protrusions – known in the trade as **'rock facing'**. 'Rock facing' is often found in combination with a deliberate refusal to arrange the stones in neat horizontal rows, in spite of (or perhaps because of) technological improvements that had made this fairly straightforward: see below under 'Arrangement of the stones used'. Not all buildings of the late Victorian and Edwardian periods were given this spuriously 'rustic' appearance of course, and many perpetuated the Regency taste for surfaces that did not merely aspire to be perfectly smooth, but actually were.

Left.
Tool marks, 1800

Right.
Rock facing, 1906

Vermicular
rustication

A much earlier expression of the impulse that led to 'rock facing' can be seen in a few monumental buildings from the seventeenth century onwards. Known as **'vermicular rustication'**, this is more or less a parody of tool marks, as if they had been made by some mythological giant. This surface technique is almost always found in bold horizontal bands, between which the surface has been made very smooth by way of contrast. All this being said, it should be remembered that once it had been invented, a given surface treatment tended not to fall out of use entirely.

2. *Size of the stones used, and the uniformity of their size.* Where this can be discerned at all – usually due to the removal of harling – buildings from before 1750 generally show a marked increase in the size of the walling stones as one looks from the top to the bottom. Compare, for instance, the stones at the bottom of the drainpipe on p. 160, to those higher up. In buildings that are older and/or built for defence, this size difference from top to bottom is even more pronounced. This was sensible enough in an era before powered hoists and

cranes, when everything had to be carried as high as necessary by human or animal power.

As the rage for symmetry intensified after 1750, however, stones were cut to a more uniform size; and in this particular field, the Victorians made no serious attempt to 'turn the clock back'. Towards the end of the 1840–1920 period, stones of a variety of sizes were again used; but this tended to be in repeating patterns such as the famous '**Aberdeen bond**' whose stones, though varying in themselves, did not change in size between the ground floor and the top floor of a given building. 'Aberdeen bond', where the smaller stones are the size of bricks, should not be confused with a largely pre-1750 practice in which the joints between the main stones are outlined in small pebbles called 'pinnings'. By 1660–1750 most 'pinnings' were merely a 'look'; but in previous eras when the main stones used were generally both larger and more shapeless, the pinnings actually formed a kind of primitive scaffolding that supported the wall structurally whilst the mortar was drying. Unaware of this, many restorers of rubble-built walls replace old mortar and pinnings with mortar only, which not only reduces the structural integrity of the wall but makes its joints appear implausibly wide.

Aberdeen bond

3. *Colours of the stones used and the uniformity of their colours.* In the era before 1750 when most buildings were harled, colour contrasts (where desired) were easily achieved simply by changing the pigment of the harling. If the visible stonework was pink, the harling might be white, but if the stones were dark grey, the harling could

be pink, and so forth. Entombed beneath the harling, stones might be of any colour, ranging from nearly white sandstone to nearly black whinstone within the space of a few feet. But after 1750, as we have seen, wealthier Scots abandoned harling. The colour of a building was now nothing more or less than the colour of its masonry. From 1750 to 1840, therefore, an expensive and fine building tended to be made up of stones of a more-or-less uniform colour, where a cheaper building will be more multi-coloured (albeit not in any particular pattern). This preference also affected the size of the joints between stones, which the builders of expensive buildings sought to minimise.

After 1840 and especially after 1880, however, many buildings, including some of the finest, were built using two or more types of stone of radically different colours – a combination of red and yellow being a particularly popular choice around 1900. This was not higgledy-piggledy as before, but highly systematic, usually with the lighter colour applied to doorways and window-surrounds, and the darker colour used for the walls themselves.

All stone is vulnerable to air pollution. Sandstone in particular is often so hard-hit by a combination of smog and rain-erosion that it has to be replaced altogether. An **apparently random pattern of 'black' and light-beige stones** in a 1750–1840 building that one would expect to be of a more uniform colour has probably undergone recent heavy-duty restoration.

4. *Outer shapes of the stones used, and the uniformity of their shapes.* As with uniformity of size, cut stones of the period 1750–1840 saw an increasing regularity and uniformity of their outer shape. And again, the Victorians made no serious efforts to undo this, despite their

Refurbished
and original
sandstone

superficial preference for pre-1660 style in most areas. Proceeding backwards in time, the stones used other than in churches and royal palaces become rougher and rougher, and even expert architectural jargoneers are forced to use genuinely descriptive terms such as 'roughly squared', 'random rubble', 'field-gatherings' and 'boulders'. 'Rock facing', a half-hearted attempt to re-create these early forms in the machine age and using machines, presents an almost disturbing contrast between the rigid rectilinearity of the stones' outer shape, and their faces hacked and hammered so as to resemble the mountains of the moon.

5. *Arrangement of the stones used.* A great deal of this, including 'pinning' and 'Aberdeen bond', has necessarily been touched upon in the sections immediately above. The main additional fact to remember is that, leaving aside the very finest buildings, there was a relatively slow and steady historical progression over the whole of the sixteenth through nineteenth centuries: from

Left.
Genuinely
random rubble
construction

Right.
Bogus
randomness

genuinely random aesthetic arrangements (which were nevertheless carefully considered from a structural point of view); to highly uniform arrangements; to **faux-random** arrangements. Uniform and faux-random arrangements both remain popular, but both look set to be surpassed by the dramatic resurgence of harling, not necessarily over stone. A combination of rising labour costs, rising cost of materials and environmental considerations dictates that many more Scottish buildings (harled or not) will henceforth be built principally of clay blocks or of wood.

Notes

1 The villain responsible for this state of affairs, according to Cézanne, was 'the Chief Engineer of Roads': Ulrike Becks-Malorny, *Cézanne* (Cologne, 2004), p. 20.

2 The idea that the Act of Union of 1707 was a fundamental watershed in Scottish architecture is particularly absurd. See John G. Dunbar, *The Historic Architecture of Scotland* (London, 1966), p. 81.

3 Scotland's first and oldest royal palace per se is Linlithgow, built 1424–28.

4 This is technically known as 'ashlar' regardless of the type of stone used.

5 Thirteenth-century Bothwell Castle in Lanarkshire and fourteenth-century Doune Castle in Stirlingshire would have been others, but neither was completed to its original plan.

6 As a very rough guide, the 'Dark Ages' begin in 400 AD and last until 800; the 'Early Middle Ages' (also coincidentally the Viking Age) are 800–1100; the 'High Middle Ages' are 1100–1350 (i.e., ending with the Black Death); and the 'Late Middle Ages' from 1350 until the discovery of America (1492–97) or the Protestant Reformation (1517–60), according to one's personal preference. Outside Scotland, the Romanesque style first emerged in the Early Middle Ages, and Gothic in the High Middle Ages.

7 Miles Glendinning and Aonghus MacKechnie, *Scottish Architecture* (London, 2004), p. 45. Scotland was 'a very minor player in the world of medieval Gothic', ibid., p. 34.

8 *Old Statistical Account* of 1791–99 (hereafter 'OSA') for the parish of Deskford.

9 Even in such ports, however, roofing tiles might also be made: in Musselburgh, East Lothian, they were manufactured beginning in the 1780s and sold throughout the surrounding area, where they are still unusually prevalent.

10 Robert J. Naismith, *Buildings of the Scottish Countryside* (London, 1985), p. 34.

11 An important later exception is the Edinburgh City Chambers, built 1753–61 as the Royal Exchange to a design by John Adam and his brother Robert Adam. This is illus. on p. 133.

12 Dunbar, *Historic Architecture*, pp. 68 and 77–78.

13 We easily forget that France nearly became a Protestant or even Presbyterian country via a series of bloody wars fought from 1562–98, their progress followed with intense interest by Protestants in Britain and elsewhere. Mercantile, academic, and familial contact between the French and Scots of both religions was, moreover, never really interrupted until the French Revolutionary and Napoleonic Wars of 1793–1815.

14 There is no information on this Wallace's relationship (if any) to the thirteenth-century military hero of the same name.

15 *Theatrum Scotiae*, printed seven times between 1693 and 1814.

16 *Oxford Dictionary of National Biography*.

17 John Summerson's argument that Bruce stamped Scotland with an English style spectacularly puts the cart before the horse. See *Architecture in Britain, 1530–1830, Vol. 3* (London, 1993), p. 510.

18 These included Burlington House and 31–34 Great Burlington Street, London (all 1718–24), of which number 32 was Campbell's own house. He died in London in 1729.

19 A.J. Youngson, *The Making of Classical Edinburgh 1750–1840* (Edinburgh, 1993 {1966}), p. 290.

20 Britain's first 'unified house frontages', i.e. terraces, are often said to have been the 'innovation' of John Wood the Elder in Bath, Somerset, particularly between 1741 and his death in the early 1750s – though the builders of Edinburgh did not wait long in following suit: Youngson, *Classical Edinburgh*, p. 95. Professor Youngson estimates that only 60 per cent of the houses in Charlotte Square were built 'by people who intended to live in them', i.e., that 40 per cent of the square was built speculatively; and further, that in less fashionable (but still expensive) parts of the New Town, the percentage of speculators was even higher. Ibid., p. 223.

21 The confused yearnings of architects and planners on the eve of full-blown 'retro' are exemplified by an 1826 paper co-written by Burn. Ostensibly a scheme to preserve the character of the Old Town, it proposed that Edinburgh High Street's remaining authentic half-timbered Jacobean townhouses be replaced by new houses 'in the old Flemish style' (quoted in Youngson,

Classical Edinburgh, p. 175). Later in the century this was actually done, e.g. at 453–463 Lawnmarket in 1892.

22 By the 1830s, the question of whether Neo-Classical or Neo-Gothic architecture was 'better' had become a subject of public debate in most European countries. This is sometimes recollected as 'The Battle of the Styles'. In Britain, Neo-Gothic can be said to have won the battle by 1840, when a Neo-Gothic design replaced the old Houses of Parliament (which had burned in 1834).

23 In this context, the Scottishness of the pan-British Neo-Classicism of 1660–1840 (see above) should be considered vis-à-vis the overwhelming Englishness of the founding generation of the Arts and Crafts movement.

24 The Institute of the Architects of Scotland (now Royal Incorporation of Architects in Scotland) was founded in 1840, and it was only after this date that the great majority of architects received formal training.

25 There was one authentically Victorian and Scottish style of building which, for want of a better term, we can call the 'giant cottage'. Its chief characteristic is external woodwork that cannot fairly be described as mock-Tudor, and which often includes rough-hewn log columns, and/or finely turned elements reminiscent of an old ship's steering wheel. In the Highlands especially, this woodwork can also take on a Scandinavian flavour. Its categorisation as 'Jacobean' in buildings listings and in other architecture books is rather unsatisfying.

26 Often erroneously called 'Tudor style', half-timber construction was commonplace both outside the Tudor period (1485–1603), and outside the realms the Tudors ruled (England, southeastern Ireland, Wales and Calais). Unfortunately, perhaps, Scotland's landowners tended to rebuild in stone the moment funds to do so became available. All the half-timber buildings you can see in Scotland are therefore 'retro' creations of the Victorian era and later, with most dating from 1890 to 1910. Some are better than others, of course, with All Saints Church in Glencarse (1878) being one of the finer examples, and Callander's Temperance Hotel one of the most jarringly bad.

27 The archetypal Victorian chair is an implausible copy, albeit a large and comfortable one, of a small, uncomfortable Baroque chair from the late Stuart period (1660–1714).

28 Specifically, Macgibbon and Ross's *The Castellated and Domes-*

tic Architecture of Scotland from the Twelfth to the Eighteenth Century (5 vols., Edinburgh, 1887); Billings's *Baronial and Ecclesiastical Antiquities of Scotland* (4 vols., Edinburgh, 1848–52; reprinted in 2 vols by Birlinn Ltd in 2008); and Gillespie's *Details of Scottish Domestic Architecture: A Series of Selected Examples from the Sixteenth and Seventeenth Centuries* (Edinburgh, 1922).

29 Ironically, the 'inside out' principle is now widely ascribed to the Arts and Crafts movement co-founded by Pugin's hated rival, John Ruskin (1819–1900) – though the differences between the two men's views were perhaps always smaller than Ruskin made out.

30 Nikolaus Pevsner, *Pioneers of Modern Design* (Harmondsworth, 1975), p. 90.

31 The third was an Englishman, Sir Arthur Lasenby Liberty, owner of Liberty & Co., due to whose influence the style is known in Italian not as 'arte nuovo' but as 'stile Liberty'.

32 Who, it should be noted, now make up an absolute majority of the population, having passed 50 per cent in the mid 1970s and 65 per cent in 2010.

33 Referring to a shield, or a shield-and-crest combination, as a 'crest' is commonplace but completely incorrect, and will only tend to confuse the people who are most able to help you with your research.

34 Or more specifically as 'banded rustication', in cases where the grooves are mostly horizontal.

35 This is the broadest possible term for a movement that can be subdivided into Palladianism, 'Adam', Greek Revival, Regency and so forth.

36 Quotation from W.A. Brogden, *Aberdeen: An Illustrated Architectural Guide* (Edinburgh, 1998), p. 33.

37 It should be noted here that well into the twentieth century, Scotland's university professors were also given free accommodation in houses called manses, albeit ones built in a wider variety of styles, and located in urban areas.

38 Though a small handful of two-storey 'great' barns do exist, as at Craigton of Abercorn in West Lothian.

39 Johnny Scott, 'Field Notes: The Month in the Country', *The Field*, Oct. 2013, p. 39.

40 Up to half of modern-day Scots consider themselves to be of noble ancestry, probably not without some justification.

41 A henhouse is a *bothag chearc*, while a rabbit-hutch is a *bothag-coinein*.

42 However, it should be noted that long, continuous rows of single-storey cottages had also been built for farmworkers during the Improvement period of 1750–1840.

43 The RCAHMS online database, known as Canmore, is free to use and quite helpful, though not nearly as helpful as direct access to the Commission's well-organised library in Bernard Terrace, Edinburgh. If doing in-depth research on a Scottish building of any age, size or type, arranging a visit is highly recommended.

44 These figures are for the early 1690s and for the Highlands and Lowlands (excluding Edinburgh), respectively. The figure for Edinburgh at the same date was 2.0 hearths per home. See R.A. Houston, *The Population History of Britain and Ireland 1550–1750* (Cambridge, 1992), p. 17.

45 Summerson, *Architecture in Britain, 1530–1830, Vol. 3*, p. 502.

46 It was all but demolished in 1938.

47 To say 're-design' here would be to overstate how much of the original structure was left intact.

48 It is a common error, particularly in North American English, to refer to dormer windows as 'gables'.

49 *OSA* for the parish of Cullen.

50 St Andrew's Parish Church in Golspie, Sutherland (1732) is arguably the least messed-about Scottish church of the mid eighteenth century. Externally, little besides its wide door, small belfry (added 1774), and relative lack of windows distinguish it from prosperous merchants' houses of a hundred years earlier.

51 Naismith, *Buildings of the Scottish Countryside*, p. 24.

52 Also known as Gray's Close or Gardyne's House, this is in fact a much older (sixteenth-century) building with a later façade.

53 It should perhaps be mentioned in this context that Scotland had no archbishop of her own for a century and a half after the fourteenth-century Wars of Independence from England, and as such, the Archbishop of York asserted his authority over all Scottish mainland bishops until 1472 – three years after King James III declared Scotland to be not merely a kingdom but an empire. That being said, the relationship between the arched or 'imperial' crown and the lantern spire has probably been overstated by some.

54 The *New Statistical Account* of 1834–45 for the parish of Marnoch.

55 The tower of St Mary's at Dunnet in Caithness is of a similar appearance, but there is currently no consensus as to its age, with estimates ranging from 'medieval' to '*c* 1700'.

56 To call them 'transoms' is not correct, however, the transom per se being the horizontal bar separating such a window from the top of the door.

57 Michael Donnelly, *Glasgow Stained Glass: A Preliminary Study* (Kilmarnock, 1985), p. 3.

58 In England, the threshhold was lowered to seven windows in 1766, and raised again (to eight) in 1825.

59 However, Burntisland's may have been added as recently as 1822. Quadruple windows, a great rarity in any period, can be seen on the 1538 chapel block of Falkland Palace.

60 Now the Edinburgh University School of Geosciences.

61 Politically, the Regency refers to the period from 1811 to 1820, when the Prince of Wales (future King George IV) acted as de facto sovereign during and because of the apparent madness of his father, George III. But casually, and therefore architecturally, 'Regency' is often used to mean the much longer period from the outbreak of the French Revolutionary Wars in the mid 1790s to the accession of Queen Victoria in 1837.

62 William Burn and Thomas Hamilton, quoted in Youngson, *Classical Edinburgh*, p. 167.

63 Many visitors to Scotland, especially from England, casually refer to all masonry work as 'brick', but it is important to distinguish true brick – a man-made product formed in moulds and then baked in ovens – from naturally occurring stone which is shaped with tools.

Further reading

The premier resource on Scottish buildings is the RCAHMS library, located in Bernard Terrace, Edinburgh. The National Library of Scotland, George IV Bridge, Edinburgh has an almost equally strong collection, albeit more dispersed and therefore somewhat harder to use. RCAHMS's online database, called Canmore, is free and straightforward to use but often contains conflicting information from various scholars and government officials, written over a period of 150 years or more. The guidebooks commissioned by the Royal Incorporation of Architects in Scotland also contain some misleading information (alas, an inevitable feature of writing about architecture!), but at least each one speaks with a single voice. Especially if you are studying a particular region, Pevsner's Guides (published initially by Penguin and more recently by Yale University Press) will also be helpful, if resolutely technical. The various works cited in the endnotes may be taken as a list of additional recommendations.

Acknowledgements

In addition to the dedicatees of this book, I would particularly like to thank Sir Angus Farquharson of Finzean, Eleanor MacCannell, Barry Robertson, Edda Frankot, Marie Shaw, Peter Davidson, Jane Stevenson, Jane Geddes, David Walker, Hugh Salvesen, Gordon Duffy, Finlay Lockie, Kirsten McKenzie, Adam Wilkinson, Marc and Karen Ellington, Dean and Juliet MacCannell, Hugh Andrew, Vicky Dawson, Andrew Simmons, Christine Laennec, Charlotte Charlton, Kimmo Karjalainen, and Paul Dukes, as well as all the personnel of the Royal Commission on the Ancient and Historical Monuments of Scotland, Historic Scotland and the National Library of Scotland who helped or encouraged me in my research. Any errors in the book are, however, my responsibility alone.

Picture credits

Acknowledgement is made to the following for artwork which appears on the following pages:

21 © Courtesy of RCAHMS. Licensor
   www.rcahms.gov.uk
23 © RCAHMS (Image reproduced courtesy of
   J.R. Hume). Licensor www.scran.ac.uk
26 (right), 27 (right), 114, 127 (bottom),
   © Kim Traynor, CC BY-SA 3.0
27 (left), 137 © Bill Harrison, CC BY-SA 3.0
44, 143 (left) © David Walker
57 © Eoin Houston, CC BY-SA 3.0
59 (top) © Dalbera, CC BY-SA 2.0
62 © Margaret Hyland, CC BY-SA 3.0
63 © RCAHMS (Sir Basil Spence Archive).
   Licensor www.rcahms.gov.uk
65 © Christine Laennec (www.christinelaennec.co.uk)
68 © Finlay McWalter, CC BY-SA 3.0
74 (top left) © SajoR, CC BY-SA 2.5
74 (top right) © Sodacan, CC BY-SA 1.0
76 (bottom right) © Marie Shaw
77 © Nick Thompson
79 © Barbara Maliszewska, CC BY-SA 3.0 Poland
81, 92, 128 (top), 167 © Anne Burgess, CC BY-SA 2.0
82 Crown Copyright © RCAHMS. Licensor
   www.rcahms.gov.uk
84 © Alistair McMillan, CC BY-SA 3.0
87, 116 (bottom) © Jonathan Oldenbuck,
   CC BY-SA 2.5

93 © National Museums Scotland. Licensor
www.scran.ac.uk

100 Crown Copyright © RCAHMS. Licensor
www.rcahms.gov.uk

104–105, 130 (top), 141 (right) © Supergolden,
CC BY-SA 3.0

116 (top) © Nick Haynes

117 © Julia MacDonald

119 © Tom Jervis, CC BY-SA 2.0

124 © SagaciousPhil, CC BY-SA 3.0

130 (bottom) © Afmell, CC BY-SA 3.0

131 © Edinburgh College of Art. Licensor
www.scran.ac.uk

132 © Sandy Kinghorn, Cracking Design. Licensor
www.scran.ac.uk

133 (top right) © Supergolden, CC BY-SA 2.5

133 (bottom right), 162 © Kim Traynor, CC BY-SA 2.0

136 © Robert Howarth

144 © Otter, CC BY-SA 3.0

149, 151, 164 (left) © Andrew Simmons

165 © Mary Hogg and Angus Hogg, CC BY-SA 2.0

169 © National Trust for Scotland. Licensor
www.scran.ac.uk

171 © Selina Zimmermann

177 Peter Ward, CC BY-SA 2.0

179 © David Langan

Making your own observations

The following pages contain a series of tables that will help you to assess particular Scottish buildings that you are interested in. Like the preceding chapters, the rows are organised in a 'top-down' format, beginning with roof features and proceeding toward ground level. The columns, meanwhile, are arranged chronologically: with the earliest features at the left and the most recent at the right. Please note, however, that while these tables overlap strongly with the content of this book so far, they are not merely a summary of its earlier sections, but contain significant information that is not mentioned elsewhere.

When using the tables, the reader should bear in mind that there are exceptions to every rule, especially since total exterior remodelling has been fairly common in Scotland over the years. As such, the full story of any Scottish building – to the extent it can ever be known – will only be achieved via a combination of access to its interior and library research. A list of additional resources is therefore provided under 'Further Reading', p. 193.

I hope that this book has already enhanced your enjoyment of Scotland's remarkable built environment, and that you will use it 'in the field' with great success in the days and months to come.

UP TO 1540	1540–1660	1660–1750	1750–1840	1840–1920	1920 ONWARD
OVERALL HEIGHT					
Can be very high, but only structures built for the well-to-do have survived. Church steeples were frequently very tall. Most people lived in single-storey houses of clay, unmortared fieldstone, or turf (in various combinations). The distinctions were minimal between such houses and inns, workshops and barns. Retail shops did not yet exist.	The earliest mortared-stone farmhouses, ministers' manses, lairds' townhouses, and lairds' unfortified rural mansions are from this period; almost none are taller than three storeys. Many parishes had no building over two storeys, though blocks of flats in Edinburgh were already reaching heights of eight storeys and more, with six being normal there. Tower-houses in the far north of Scotland tended to be taller and thinner than those elsewhere. Squat, house-like bell-towers adorned a minority of churches, but true steeples were not generally constructed. The new retail shops constructed after 1660 and particularly after 1720 might be of one to four storeys, with two storeys probably usual.		A quantum leap in ceiling height occurs at the beginning of this period, making a given building typically 30 per cent taller than one from the previous period with the same number of floors. Steeples return to church construction after a 200-year absence. Blocks of flats in Edinburgh still routinely reach heights of six storeys, though five storeys is considered unusually tall elsewhere. The average height of commercial buildings increases steadily, due to the emergence of three-storey-plus factories, banks, and hotels, later joined by theatres, department stores and pubs. At the end of this period, Dundee has the most expensive real estate in the world, and perhaps unsurprisingly the highest ceilings in Scotland. Beverly Hills, California surpasses Dundee in price only in the late 1920s.		Steeple-building wanes, and suburban houses are increasingly likely to be single-storey rather than two or three storeys. Post-WWII 'Brutalism', however, emphasises height: social housing, barracks, and office blocks attain sizes only previously achieved by cathedrals. However, the heights of Brutalist high-rises' individual storeys may be shorter than at any time since 1750.

UP TO 1540	1540–1660	1660–1750	1750–1840	1840–1920	1920 ONWARD
CHIMNEY STACKS (NOBILITY)					
Massive stacks, often rather shapeless or with poorly defined 'shoulders'.	Previous style continues. From 1600, we also see thin, square, single-flue stacks, usually in groups of two or more and angled at 45 degrees to the foot-print of the house.	Rectangles with 'coved' tops, containing two to four flues apiece, are usual in all gables (including directly over front doors).	Wide, plain stacks containing four flues or more are usual for dwellings; hotels, banks and blocks of flats have many more flues (often more than twenty) but still generally accommodated within a single stack at each end. A chimney above the front door is increasingly rare, being replaced in gentry houses by classical pediments (if anything).	All previous styles except wooden flues are continued or revived. Rectangular stacks of 1750–1840 type are, however, now often built in brick. Single-flue stacks on a small building now generally indicate that it is intended for a lone occupant e.g. a watchman or caretaker, and/or that it is only used during the day.	All previous styles except those with wooden flues are continued or revived.
CHIMNEY STACKS (OTHERS)					
Non-noble houses of this date are unlikely to survive. Chimneys often consisted merely of a single wooden flue suspended directly from roofing material.	Previous style continues, but square stone stacks (usually not at a 45-degree angle to the footprint of the house) are seen on those non-noble buildings that are built in stone. Two to three thin stacks usually indicates a dwelling; one fat stack, a workshop or bakery; no stacks, a storage facility or barn.				Use of chimneys of any type decreases due to changes in heating and cooking technology.

UP TO 1540	1540–1660	1660–1750	1750–1840	1840–1920	1920 ONWARD

CHIMNEY POTS

UP TO 1540	1540–1660	1660–1750	1750–1840	1840–1920	1920 ONWARD
None (barring later additions).		Rare (and may be later additions).	Usual for buildings of all types and classes.	Usual, except in 'retro' replications of previous, potless styles.	Usual in Neo-Georgian 'retro' buildings; otherwise rare.

ROOF RIDGES

UP TO 1540	1540–1660	1660–1750	1750–1840	1840–1920	1920 ONWARD
Most original roofs were of thatch, turf, wooden planks or solid stone slabs. Slate roofs that have been applied retrospectively usually have ridges of lead or slate.		First original slate roofs for the nobility only, with lead or slate ridges. Thatch, turf and timber still normal for others, though slate will have been applied retrospectively to buildings of all sorts.	Slate roofs with lead or slate ridges now usual for all classes and locations.	Terracotta ridges popular, but lead and slate continue.	Terracotta ridges again rarer than lead and slate, but are still seen, especially down to 1950.

ROOFING MATERIAL

UP TO 1540	1540–1660	1660–1750	1750–1840	1840–1920	1920 ONWARD
Slate is to be expected, though hardly ever original. Most original roofs were of thatch, turf, wooden planks or solid stone slabs.		Slate may be original, or a replacement for thatch, etc. Composite tile-and-slate roofs, with the slate courses nearest the ground, are frequently seen on Southeast Scottish shops from c.1700–1750.		Slate usual, and mostly original, but thatch still applied to new buildings in remote rural areas.	Use of slate dwindles due to increasing use of flat roofs and synthetic alternatives. New building using thatch ceases.

UP TO 1540	1540–1660	1660–1750	1750–1840	1840–1920	1920 ONWARD

CROWSTEPS

UP TO 1540 / 1540–1660 / 1660–1750	1750–1840	1840–1920	1920 ONWARD
Reasonably likely to be found on buildings of all regions, costs, and purposes. May be found most popular in the Southeast of Scotland. May be found on just one gable of a two-gabled building, but never on dormers in this period. 'Flights' of crowsteps may pierce the centre of a roof as the upward continuation of an interior wall. Steps may be of differing heights within a single 'flight'. Two 'flights' may join the same chimney-stack at different heights above the ground. Smooth-surfaced examples are rare.	Almost never used.	Reasonably likely to be found on buildings of all regions, costs, and purposes. Unlikely to be found on just one gable of a two-gabled building. Very frequently used on dormers in this period. 'Flights' unlikely to pierce the centre of a roof as the upward continuation of an interior wall. Steps tend to be very smooth and even, and front and back 'flights' are highly likely to join a chimney-stack at the same height above the ground. Most post-1840 examples are about 50 per cent larger than their pre-1750 forebears.	No pattern, as all previous styles are continued or revived, particularly after c.1870.

ANGLE OF NORMAL PEAKED ROOF

UP TO 1540	1540–1660	1660–1750	1750–1840	1840–1920	1920 ONWARD
Highly variable (even within a given building), but on average around 90 degrees.	Steep: 60 to 80 degrees.	Steepness declines gradually, from 60–80 degrees at the beginning of the period to 80–90 degrees at the end.	Steepness continues declining gradually, from 90 degrees at the beginning of the period to 100 degrees at the end.		

UP TO 1540	1540–1660	1660–1750	1750–1840	1840–1920	1920 ONWARD

ANY ROOFS IN TRUNCATED-PYRAMID OR 'HIPPED' / 'PIEND' SHAPE?

UP TO 1540	1540–1660	1660–1750	1750–1840	1840–1920	1920 ONWARD
No.		Yes (especially for gentry and professional classes); usually shallow i.e. with sides at 45 degrees from the horizontal or less.		Yes. Previous style continues, but extremely tall/steep truncated pyramids are very popular 1860s–80s.	Yes; no longer restricted to gentry, and even used on social housing of the 1920s–30s.

ANY ROOFS IN 'OGEE' SHAPE?

UP TO 1540	1540–1660	1660–1750	1750–1840	1840–1920	1920 ONWARD
No, or extremely rare.	Yes. Extremely popular 1590–1640.	No, or extremely rare.		Yes. Revived as an element of 'Scots Baronial' style.	

ANY ROOFS THAT APPEAR TO BE FLAT WHEN VIEWED FROM THE GROUND?

UP TO 1540	1540–1660	1660–1750	1750–1840	1840–1920	1920 ONWARD
Only on castles and castellated church towers.		Only on the palaces of the higher nobility.	Use in 'palatial' country houses continues, but the look is increasingly common, especially in urban areas. It retains an increasingly tenuous status as a mark of high quality and distinction.		The connection between the flat roof and costliness is broken, as it becomes a signature feature of the Art Deco style of 1920–40, and is used for commercial and civic buildings of all styles and quality levels.

FORTIFICATIONS INCLUDING CRENELLATIONS, BARTIZANS, SHOT-HOLES AND ARROW SLITS

UP TO 1540	1540–1660	1660–1750	1750–1840	1840–1920	1920 ONWARD
Are legitimate. 'Bartizans' (small corner turrets) tend to lack roofs.	Are becoming stylistic hangovers, but still have some utility due to the primitive state of military technology. Bartizans more likely to have roofs. Last true castles constructed.	Are absolutely abnormal; only one arguable mock-castle built (Lochryan, Wigtownshire, 1701).	Are a major sub-theme of the period's aristocratic architecture, especially from 1770 to 1820, though most buildings – including aristocratic buildings in the cities – remain almost totally unaffected.	Are commonplace once again, as the style of 1540–1660 is widely replicated, not just for houses but for hotels, train stations, etc.	Are once more almost as rare as they were between 1660 and 1750, though from the 1930s onward we have seen a tiny number of plausible fake tower-houses constructed in a c.1600 style.

DORMERS

UP TO 1540	1540–1660	1660–1750	1750–1840	1840–1920	1920 ONWARD
Wallhead dormers are relatively few; most could have been added later. Non-wallhead dormers prevalent on church steeples but in few other settings.	Wallhead dormers – either pointed or 'cat-slide' – are the normal type of upper-storey window in this period, though some non-wallhead dormers are also constructed.	Original dormers of any type are rare in this period. However, many structures of this date have had post-1840 bay-fronted dormers inserted.	Wallhead dormers virtually unknown. A few non-wallhead dormers (rectangular or drum-shaped) appear, mostly in fashionable urban areas.	All previous styles of dormer are continued or revived – frequently at a larger overall size than their predecessors of the same style. The stone frames of 'retro' wallhead dormers are generally wider (>15") than those of the originals (<15"). Crowstepped dormers are popular for the first time.	

WALLING MATERIALS

UP TO 1540	1540–1660	1660–1750	1750–1840	1840–1920	1920 ONWARD
Only the stone-built structures of the wealthy and powerful survive. Those of the crown and church make use of the costly, edged masonry known generically as 'ashlar'; those of the merely noble are built of rubble and coated with harling.	Some stone construction by middle classes, but most still use 'mud' (clay) or half-timber techniques. Most stone structures and some clay ones are harled. The building of royal residences and cathedrals ceases, so ashlar is generally seen only on window-surrounds, chimney-stack edges, and other decorative details.	Last uses of clay by the middle classes; first uses of mortared stone by the labouring classes. Harling still poor. Harling work normal, though work on un-harled royal palaces recommences after 1670. In place of rubble, stones are now mostly carved into rough rectangular blocks and laid in approximately level horizontal courses, even when harling is to be applied.	Stone now used by all classes, with ashlar being extensively adopted by the upper and upper-middle classes. First extensive uses of brick and iron, initially mostly in residences. Harling falls out of favour with the upper classes at the beginning of the period, and with all classes by the end.	Ashlar used by all classes – though intentionally distressed ('rock-faced') stone is equally popular after 1880. Concrete walls used for the first time (chiefly by the rural poor); first use of glossy tile (chiefly by the urban middle classes). Harling is virtually unknown even in 'retro' structures. Brick and iron used more extensively and in large commercial buildings. Often in combination with 'rock-facing', stones are now often laid in non-horizontal repeating patterns rather than in level courses.	Rapidly increasing use of brick, iron/steel and concrete at the expense of stone. Harling is rediscovered and re-popularised, often to add a veneer of tradition to buildings made largely of these non-traditional structural materials. Very recent experimental reintroductions of timber, clay, and compressed earth walls have also occurred.

UP TO 1540	1540–1660	1660–1750	1750–1840	1840–1920	1920 ONWARD

WINDOW APERTURES

UP TO 1540	1540–1660	1660–1750	1750–1840	1840–1920	1920 ONWARD
Approximately equal numbers of small vertical rectangles, squares, and slits, with the odd horizontal rectangle sometimes seen, especially on ground floors. Small round holes may be gun-ports for pistols, though in inhabited houses these will now mostly be glassed-in. Gothic-pointed windows generally only found in churches and schools.	Almost all are small vertical rectangles, but with the occasional small square (particularly high up in gable ends) and/or horizontal oval, circle, or triangle (particularly above front doors). Round-topped windows including 'Venetian' windows are mostly from after 1725.	Vertical rectangles – often round-topped – still dominate, but are larger than previously, especially after 1800 when steam power is introduced to glass-making. Some squares and horizontal rectangles in attics and basements of the well-to-do. Large, square, non-opening, often convex multi-paned windows may be original shop windows from this period or the next. First widespread use of Gothic pointed windows in residential buildings.	All previous styles are continued or revived, albeit at the larger scale implied by post-1750 increases in ceiling height and post-1800 improvements in glass manufacture. Giant half-circular windows (round part upward) are characteristic of industrial and civic architecture from this period, especially after 1880.	Horizontal rectangles tend to dominate within the Art Deco movement of 1920–40 (though their absence should not be seen as proof that a building is not Art Deco). Post-war 'Brutalism' usually characterised either by dense, closely packed ranks of very narrow vertical rectangles, or else an apparently random mixture of horizontal rectangles and squares.

WINDOW FITTINGS

UP TO 1540	1540–1660	1660–1750	1750–1840	1840–1920	1920 ONWARD
Originally, dozens of tiny panes (diamond-shaped, triangular and/or circular) bound together with lead. Now, expect to see sash-and-case replacements of four to twenty-eight panes, according to the size and shape of the window.		The first original sash-and-case windows date from the early part of this period, and tend to have eight to twelve small panes and thick glazing bars.	Sash-and-case windows of twelve panes (i.e. three wide by four high) are firmly established as normal. The size of the glass increases dramatically over this period, both in absolute terms and relative to the thickness of the glazing bars.	Surprisingly, pre-sash window styles (other than stained glass) are not revived – effectively crowning the sash window as the 'normal' Scottish window for buildings of all styles and time periods. However, the number of panes in a sash window varies sharply: windows over six feet high but with only two or four panes in total are frequently seen 1840–80. Particularly in the new suburbs, after 1880 and as late as 1950, sash windows with a different number of panes in the top half (usually eight or more) and the bottom half (one or two) are also popular.	Decreasing use of sash windows except in 'retro' building and conservation projects. New window fittings are mostly hinged at one side, and frequently made of steel before the Second World War and of plastics afterwards. Windows consisting of a single pane are increasingly common. However, a reaction in favour of the traditional sash window (or at least its look) is in full swing, and many experiments with energy-efficient wooden sash windows are ongoing.

UP TO 1540	1540–1660	1660–1750	1750–1840	1840–1920	1920 ONWARD

WINDOW ARRANGEMENTS (GENERAL)

UP TO 1540	1540–1660	1660–1750	1750–1840	1840–1920	1920 ONWARD
No readily discernible patterns, except that for reasons of defensibility, large windows (if indeed there are any) tend to be placed at greater heights from the ground.	A minority of buildings that would have been considered 'fashionable' have some groups of windows arranged in rows and columns, but these are far from tidy.	For residences, rigid symmetry in window arrangements becomes normal. Windows should generally align both vertically and horizontally, and frame doorways neatly and evenly. Untidy window arrangements may therefore be a sign that a building from this period was built as a shop, inn, coffeehouse, barracks, etc. rather than as a dwelling. It may even be a clue to unsuspected earlier origins.		Asymmetry rules again, as 'retro' replication of pre-1660 architecture takes pride of place in Scottish architecture. However, Georgian notions of symmetry linger in rural areas and less expensive urban ones where building is still done 'by eye' rather than at the direction of professional architects.	Neither pre-war Art Deco nor post-war Brutalism take a strong stand on the symmetry vs. asymmetry debate. Neo-Georgian architecture of 1920–40 is by and large as symmetrical as the 1660–1840 architecture it is copying, but this goes, well, out the window after the Second World War. Symmetry appears to remain a fairly low priority for builders in all current styles, 'retro' or otherwise.

UP TO 1540	1540–1660	1660–1750	1750–1840	1840–1920	1920 ONWARD

WINDOW PAIRS

UP TO 1540 / 1540–1660	1660–1750	1750–1840	1840–1920	1920 ONWARD
Only a handful of surviving examples are known. These may have been hangovers or revivals of twelfth-century Church architecture.	No deliberate examples known.	A tiny number of examples were built as part of the 'mock-castle' trend of the 1770s–1820s, but these windows did not spread to other sorts of buildings, with the exception of Burntisland Parish Church as remodelled in 1822.	Increasingly popular throughout the period, and dominant from the 1880s through 1940s in buildings that aspired to a 'traditional' style.	

WINDOW TRIOS

UP TO 1540	1840–1920
Only a handful of examples are known.	Almost as popular as window pairs between 1890 and 1910, but fairly rare after the First World War.

UP TO 1540	1540–1660	1660–1750	1750–1840	1840–1920	1920 ONWARD

SEGMENTAL OR 'HUMP-TOPPED' ARCHES

UP TO 1540	1540–1660	1660–1750	1750–1840	1840–1920	1920 ONWARD
Commonplace for doors and pends, but for windows, Stirling Castle may be the only example.		No longer used for doors. House of Gray near Dundee has extremely rare example of windows. Commonly used for pends.	Use for pends continues. Fairly commonly used on windows, but only in basement areas. No doors, but certain fanlights give a segmentally arched appearance to their doorway taken as a whole.	Popular window type from 1880, and extremely popular 1900–20, especially in urban working-class housing, factories, technical schools, and so forth. Use as a door shape does not resume, however, and pends are now seldom built.	Infrequently seen in any context. New pends are mostly square-topped.

DOOR SIZE

UP TO 1540	1540–1660	1660–1750	1750–1840	1840–1920	1920 ONWARD
Generally 7' high or less, except for churches, royal palaces and the mansions of the higher nobility. Double doors in public buildings only.			Height generally increases to 8' or more, not including the transom windows that now appear above most residential front doors for the first time. Double doors are widely used in residences for the first time.	Increased door height and transom windows persist from the preceding period, though double doors are used less frequently in houses.	Door height decreases along with ceiling height, especially in less costly buildings.

UP TO 1540	1540–1660	1660–1750	1750–1840	1840–1920	1920 ONWARD

DOOR CONSTRUCTION

UP TO 1540	1540–1660	1660–1750	1750–1840	1840–1920	1920 ONWARD
Thick wood, usually reinforced with iron, visible on the exterior face in the form of multiple studs, rivets or bolt-heads. These may be in a regular pattern, e.g. diamonds, or in no obvious pattern. Many have viewing-hatches at approximately face height, and where provided, these hatches are usually covered with iron grilles. Iron grilles covering the whole door, known as 'yetts', were outlawed in 1606 but many remained in place, and new ones continued to appear down to the end of the period.		Generally of a thinner, plainer construction than previously, and often brightly painted rather than left in a natural wood colour. Iron reinforcements and viewing-hatches are now quite rare, but alternative types of in-door windows and other decoration (e.g. brass knockers) have yet to appear.	The standard 'modern' type of door constructed of rectangular panels surrounded by hemispherical mouldings, usually with a knocker and often with a letter-flap, moves rapidly from aristocratic use at the beginning of the period to general use by the end. Almost all doors are still painted, but usually in more sober colours, especially black.	All previous styles are continued or revived, albeit at the larger scale implied by post-1750 increases in ceiling height.	All previous styles are continued or revived. Ceiling height (and therefore door height) retreat nearly to pre-1750 levels in some housing built for the poor.

IS THE TOP OF THE MAIN DOORWAY THE SAME HEIGHT AS THE TOPS OF THE GROUND-FLOOR WINDOWS?

UP TO 1540	1540–1660	1660–1750	1750–1840	1840–1920	1920 ONWARD
Rarely.			Almost always.		As often as not.

UP TO 1540	1540–1660	1660–1750	1750–1840	1840–1920	1920 ONWARD

STEPS UP TO MAIN DOOR

UP TO 1540	1540–1660	1660–1750	1750–1840	1840–1920	1920 ONWARD
Were usually of wood and intended to be removed in time of invasion or civil conflict.	Were not generally provided; lower edges of doors tended to be level with the ground/ street. An entrance door on an upper storey, accessed by stone stairs, may indicate that a building from this period was a workshop, small factory or store-house (especially if there is an additional entrance door on the ground floor).	Stone steps up to front doors come into vogue among the aristocracy; others are mostly still flush with the ground/street.	One or more steps up to front doors are now general for all classes in most urban areas and many villages.	No clear pattern, as many builders continue the practices of 1750–1840 while as many others attempt to replicate the step-less styles of 1540–1660.	As with the case of symmetry vs. asymmetry in window arrangements (see above), designers from the past 100 years have exhibited no clear consensus on whether steps to front doors should be provided.

MULTIPLE EXTERIOR DOORS VISIBLE FROM FRONT / STREET SIDE

UP TO 1540	1540–1660	1660–1750	1750–1840	1840–1920	1920 ONWARD
Are unusual but not especially significant.		Usually indicate a civic or commercial building.	The first semi-detached and terraced houses appear, though small civic, commercial and industrial buildings may also still have multiple doors.	Semis and terraces proliferate, whilst purpose-built retail premises are now more likely to have a single door flanked by display windows. Theatres and secular public lecture halls, both of which proliferate in this period, often have multiple sets of double doors.	

UP TO 1540	1540–1660	1660–1750	1750–1840	1840–1920	1920 ONWARD
EXTERNAL IRONWORK (OTHER THAN DOORKNOBS)					
Likely to include defensive grilles over doors; studs in doors; defensive grilles over observation hatches in doors; light artillery pieces.		Not usually seen.	Door-knockers; railed-in 'areas', sometimes with integral lamp-posts; small balconies.	Columns/porticoes; whole cast-iron shop-fronts; spikes on top of gables that in previous eras were more likely to hold chimneys. Use of 'area' railings continues.	Decreasing popularity of decorative external iron-work hastened by wartime metal-collecting. Neo-Georgian houses of the 1920s–30s feature less ironwork than their forefathers of c.1800 did.
GENERAL FORM (NOBLES' RURAL RESIDENCES)					
Footprint: short rectangle or square. Height: four to six storeys normal, if 'cap-houses' are included. Few openings. Surface decoration scant.	Footprint: increasingly complex (era of the 'L' plan, 'Z' plan and so forth). Height: three to five storeys normal. Extensive use of string courses, corbelling, and heraldry for external decoration. Larger numbers of larger windows than previously.	Footprint: a long narrow rectangle. Height: two or three storeys normal. Heraldry remains prominent, but string courses and corbelling usually replaced by plainer surfaces. Number and size of windows continues to increase.	Footprint: increasing compared to previous period, generally in terms of depth; many houses now four windows deep where before two was normal and three considered generous. Heraldry largely vanishes. Number of windows at 'saturation point' but their size continues to increase.	All post-1540 styles continued or revived, albeit usually with a smaller number of taller floors: e.g. two-storey houses that are the same height in feet as a three-storey house from the seventeenth century in a superficially similar style.	All previous styles revived, generally with a more credible approach to scale than had been the case in the 1840–1920 period.

UP TO 1540	1540–1660	1660–1750	1750–1840	1840–1920	1920 ONWARD

GENERAL FORM (OTHERS' RURAL RESIDENCES)

UP TO 1540	1540–1660	1660–1750	1750–1840	1840–1920	1920 ONWARD
Footprint: often round or oval, but too few survive to make generalisations worthwhile. Height: one storey the norm.	Footprint: pictorial evidence suggests that round/oval shapes were still frequently seen. However, some rectangular two-storey farmhouses and manses were built and survive. Cottages of the labouring poor still of one storey.			Footprint: deep rectangular stone farmhouses and manses of two storeys are now normal. The classic 'but and ben' one-storey rectangular cottage evolves in this period from earlier, round-cornered designs. However, many rural labourers are now housed in purpose-built terraces (some of two storeys) and bothies.	Newly built rural houses are increasingly unlikely to differ from their suburban counterparts, though conversion of barns amounting almost to reconstruction continues on a large scale.

GENERAL FORM (URBAN RESIDENCES)

UP TO 1540	1540–1660	1660–1750	1750–1840	1840–1920	1920 ONWARD
Footprint: rectangular or square, with short rectangles being most usual. Height: two to four storeys normal outside Edinburgh, where 'tenements' were commonplace. Nobles' townhouses were generally of stone, with similar defensive or mock-defensive features as rural castles. Others' urban houses were usually half-timbered, though the very poor might live in unmortared single-storey stone-and-turf huts even in the largest cities.		Footprint: mostly rectangular. Height: two to four storeys normal outside Edinburgh, where taller 'tenements' are still built. Distinctions between nobles' houses and merchants' houses disappear as defensive features lose popularity and stone construction becomes commonplace. Windows increase dramatically in numbers, size, and regularity of placement. The poor continue mostly to occupy one-storey houses, though these are increasingly likely to be of clay and/or mortared stone rather than unmortared rubble or turf.		To a lesser extent than England, Scotland sees a division of society into detached houses for the upper- and upper-middle classes, semi-detached houses for the middle-middle and lower-middle classes, and terraced houses for the working classes. Footprints and heights of these houses vary dramatically according to their style, though the working classes generally make do with two storeys or fewer, and the upper classes three storeys or more. This persists after 1920, but is complicated by the greatly increased popularity of flats among all classes. Many old houses, former factories and even churches and castles are converted into flats.	

UP TO 1540	1540–1660	1660–1750	1750–1840	1840–1920	1920 ONWARD

GENERAL FORM (SHOPS)

UP TO 1540	1540–1660	1660–1750	1750–1840	1840–1920	1920 ONWARD
None existed. Goods were stored in merchants' own homes and sold in the open air at market crosses, fairs, and wharves.	Purpose-built shops and pubs, especially from 1720–1800, tended to have a frontage of four windows, two or three front doors, and a centred frontal gable with a width of two windows. Inns and coffeehouses were more likely to resemble houses, but most have more irregular window arrangements than dwellings of the same age.			The modern form of shop with large display window(s), often built as a single-storey, flat-roofed extension of a taller, older building, becomes dominant. It is joined by multi-storey department stores and other larger establishments, particularly after 1880. Also from 1880, a small shop situated on the corner of two streets (or a street and an alley) was likely to be entered via a door in a 'cut-off' corner.	

PRINCIPAL FOREIGN INFLUENCES (IN ROUGH ORDER OF IMPORTANCE)

UP TO 1540	1540–1660	1660–1750	1750–1840	1840–1920	1920 ONWARD
French, Flemish, Italian.	Danish, French, English.	Dutch, English, Swedish.	Ancient Roman; sixteenth-century Italian; Ancient Greek; medieval English.	Scottish of 1540–1660; English of 1200s–1600s; contemporary French.	Contemporary North American; Scottish / British of 1750–1840.

UP TO 1540	1540–1660	1660–1750	1750–1840	1840–1920	1920 ONWARD

PALLADIAN STYLE

UP TO 1540	1540–1660	1660–1750	1750–1840	1840–1920	1920 ONWARD
Did not exist.	Existed, but was not used in Scotland.	Was introduced to Scotland but only for the houses of great noblemen (e.g. Hopetoun) and the most important civic buildings (e.g. Edinburgh's Royal Exchange).	Crept down the social scale to include some of the houses and offices of the urban professional classes, and some churches.	Descended the social scale further, to be used on police stations, banks, and theatres. Residential building in the style largely ceased.	Largely disappeared due to shortages of skilled labour and increased materials costs. The High Court of Justiciary (1934–37) in Lawnmarket, Edinburgh is a rare example, and highly influenced by Art Deco.

KEY BUILDERS / ARCHITECTS (IN ROUGH CHRONOLOGICAL ORDER)

UP TO 1540	1540–1660	1660–1750	1750–1840	1840–1920	1920 ONWARD
Few are known by name, but toward the end of this period or the beginning of the next, Conn of Auchry built four superb castles in Aberdeenshire. James Nicholson, John Scrimgeour and James Hamilton were masters of work to the crown in the 1520s and 30s.	Bel family; William Schaw; William Aitoun; William Wallace; Mylne family.	William Bruce; James Smith; Colen Campbell; William Adam.	William Chambers; Robert Adam; John Adam; William Burn.	William Burn; W.H. Playfair; Charles Rennie Mackintosh; Robert Lorimer.	Robert Lorimer; Alexander Marshall Mackenzie; Basil Spence.

REIGNS WORTH REMEMBERING

UP TO 1540	1540–1660	1660–1750	1750–1840	1840–1920	1920 ONWARD
The 'modern' church structure of parishes and cathedrals is established, and is usually if perhaps erroneously credited to King David I (r. 1124–53). The first royal palace, Linlithgow, is built for James I (r. 1406–37), and the Renaissance styles of architecture were particularly promoted by James IV (r. 1488–1513) and James V (r. 1513–42).	Danish influence is especially notable during the marriage of James VI to Anna of Denmark (which lasts from 1589–1619) and the reign of the couple's son, Charles I (crowned 1625). The Civil Wars and republican regimes of 1637–60 see much destruction and little innovation.	Charles II's return from exile in 1660 brings with it a wave of new men and new ideas. Many of King Charles's appointees continue in post beyond his death in 1685 and even past the Whig revolution of 1688–91. The advent of a new, German royal family in 1714 brings few changes, as the Scottish-led architectural establishment put in place under Charles II is already firmly entrenched in both Scotland and England.	A period nearly contiguous with the long reign of George III (r. 1760–1820), who decisively liberalises Britain in matters of religion. This leads to a far greater variety of churches, especially after 1790.	This era nearly coincides with the long reign of Victoria (r. 1837–1901). Though her personal influence on architecture is fairly minimal, she does not oppose the radically Neo-Gothic design for the new Houses of Parliament in Westminster, and later delights in the rebuilding of Balmoral Castle in a pseudo-sixteenth century style. Her attitude helps stoke the fires of 'retro' architecture throughout the period.	So many public buildings from the reign of King George V (1911–36) are constructed in a newly created Neo-Georgian style that the style itself can be seen as an homage to the king, or at least his name. The current heir to the throne is at least as keenly interested in modern and historic architecture and town planning as his predecessor and namesake Charles II.